The Newborn Christian

THE NEWBORN

114 Readings from

CHRISTIAN

J. B. PHILLIPS

Macmillan Publishing Co., Inc.

NEW YORK

ACKNOWLEDGMENT IS MADE to Harold Shaw Publishers for permission to reprint material from *Ring of Truth*, North American edition, Harold Shaw Publishers, 1977; copyright © 1967 by J. B. Phillips, Hodder & Stoughton, Ltd., London, and to the following for excerpts from other of J. B. Phillips' works, as shown:

The Methodist Publishing House, London: *Appointment with God*, copyright © 1954 by J. B. Phillips; *Plain Christianity*, copyright © 1952 by J. B. Phillips; and *Your God Is Too Small*, copyright © 1952 by J. B. Phillips;

The Highway Press, London: *Making Men Whole*, copyright © 1952 by J. B. Phillips;

Hodder & Stoughton, London: *New Testament Christianity*, copyright © 1956 by J. B. Phillips and *For This Day*, copyright © 1974 by J. B. Phillips;

Collins Publishers, London: *Four Prophets*, copyright © 1963 by J. B. Phillips and *Good News*, copyright © 1960 by J. B. Phillips.

Library of Congress Cataloging in Publication Data

Phillips, John Bertram, 1906–
    The newborn Christian.

    Bibliography: p.
    1. Meditations.   I. Title.
BV4832.2.P497   242   78-7533
ISBN 0-02-596120-9

Macmillan Publishing Co., Inc.
866 Third Avenue, New York, N.Y. 10022

First Printing 1978

Printed in the United States of America

Contents

vi   CONTENTS

CONTENTS

viii   CONTENTS

CONTENTS

Foreword

Bombs fell, sirens wailed, and buildings collapsed as J. B. Phillips talked about beatings, stonings, and shipwrecks. What first-century Christians had to endure was not unlike what twentieth-century Londoners had thrust upon them. Descriptions of the first-century experience, however, couched as they were in the regal English of the sixteenth and seventeenth centuries, were not easy for twentieth-century parishioners to understand. To remedy the situation, the London vicar decided to try his hand at Englishing one of the epistles. "It's like seeing an old picture after it's been cleaned," said C. S. Lewis about the result, and he urged the vicar to do more.

Phillips's university education and pastoral experience admirably equipped him to be a translator. He was graduated from Cambridge with an honors degree in classics and English in 1927. He was ordained a priest of the Anglican Church in 1931. He served as curate at St. John's and St. Margaret's, both churches in London, in the decade that followed. He was appointed vicar of the Church of the Good Shepherd, also in London, in 1941, and began the work that would occupy the next thirty years of his life.

Between the two curacies Phillips came down with a disabling sickness. Hospitalization and surgery followed, and when he heard a doctor tell a nurse that he would not live through the night, he did not despair. He fell into a deep sleep in which he saw "a vista of indescribable beauty." The earth breathed sweetness, and as an arrow seeks the bull's-eye, he ran toward "a white shining bridge" that would cross him from this world to the next. At the bridge's edge, however, he was met by a figure in white who gently but firmly indicated that it was not yet the fullness of his time. Phillips woke up from his dream, weeping with disappointment. The crisis was past. From that moment on his health improved, and the conviction that a special providence was at work in his life increased.

Letters to Young Churches—the title was suggested by Lewis—was published in 1947. The Acts of the Apostles was published as *The Young Church in Action* in 1955. *The Book of Revelation* appeared in 1957. *The New Testament in Modern English* was published in 1958; a second, thoroughly revised edition was published in 1972. Both editions have had sales in the millions both in England and the United States. And his only foray into the Old Testament—*Four Prophets: Amos, Hosea, First Isaiah, Micah*—was published in 1963.

Phillips's pastoral work during the years of translation also resulted in books. Bible readings appeared as *Making Men Whole* (1952). Destructive and constructive conceptions of God were dealt with in *Your God Is Too Small* (1953). Lenten addresses on the subject of Holy Communion became *Appointment with God* (1954). Talks for the British Broadcasting Corporation and the Australian Broadcasting Commission were collected under the title *Plain Christianity* (1956). Lectures in England and the United States were gathered under the title *New Testament Christianity* (1957). A series of twenty-six radio plays for the BBC had the biographical title, *A Man Called Jesus* (1959). And an anthology of various materials was called *Good News: Thoughts on God and Man* (1963).

If there is one word to describe Phillips's Christianity, it would be *newborn*. The sort of faith professed by Christians in the first century—focused, vigorous, harmonious—is exactly the sort of faith he recommends to Christians in the twentieth century. Against the attacks of avant-garde theologians and skeptical Bible scholars in the 1950s and 1960s, he stood firm. Against a religionless Christianity and a demythologized Jesus, he struck back. In *Ring of Truth*, which was published in 1967, he gave his testimony as a translator that the epistles and gospels rang true, like silver shekels flung on a marble floor.

What a newborn Christian of the first and indeed of any other century believes, therefore, is the subject of this anthology. Selections have been taken from nine of J. B. Phillips's works. The readings are thematically arranged, informally systematized, and devotionally styled. Sources of the readings are given at the back of this book.

—WILLIAM GRIFFIN
Macmillan Publishing Co., Inc.
June 1, 1978

God Unfocused

LET US FLING wide the doors and windows of our minds and make some attempt to appreciate the "size" of God. He must not be limited to religious matters or even to the "religious" interpretation of life. He must not be confined to one particular section of time nor must we imagine Him as the local god of this planet or even only of the Universe that astronomical survey has so far discovered. It is not, of course, physical size that we are trying to establish in our minds. (Physical size is not important. By any reasonable scheme of values a human being is of vastly greater worth than a mountain ten million times his physical size.) It is rather to see the immensely broad sweep of the Creator's activity, the astonishing complexity of His mental processes which science laboriously uncovers, the vast sea of what we

1

can only call "God" in a small corner of which man lives and moves and has his being.

To meditate on this broadness and vastness will do much . . . but if we stop there we may get no further than sensing a vague "unfocused" God, a depersonalized "Something" which is after a while peculiarly unsatisfying.

Spiritual Values

BY [SPIRITUAL VALUES] we mean the qualities of spirit, of personality, which are recognizable and assessable, but are incapable either of scientific weighing or measuring—and incapable of physical destruction. In the light of the probable ultimate fate of the planet and of the present (far more impressive) threat to human life, we are driven to reconsider whether after all there is reality beyond the physical, measurable reality. We begin to wonder whether the whole position is not now the reverse of what men once thought. They used to talk of the "spiritual" values as shadowy and unsubstantial, and the physical as solid and "real" and reliable. They are beginning to see that the opposite may well be true. We can certainly see evidence of the universal destructibility of matter: perhaps it is after all true that "reality" lies in another realm altogether, and that its values are not unsubstantial after all.

This, of course, is far more readily believed by some temperaments than by others. The poets, artists, and philosophers, as well as a great many other undistinguished people, of many ages, have probably been more or less acutely conscious that the "spiritual" is of vastly greater importance than the material. To all of them, speaking broadly, this present physical life is the visible and tangible stage or battlefield of spiritual forces. Universal values, such as truth, goodness, and beauty, were often considered to exist apart from, as well as being exhibited in, the life of this world. To some of them this present life is merely the prelude, lived under difficulty and handicap, to a free unfettered life of the spirit. The latter is reality—the former is an important but transitory incident.

This age-long intuition is now being forced upon humanity as a strong and workable hypothesis by the threatened disintegration of the merely physical. And there is enough inward assent to it in the hearts of most men to give them at any rate one powerful clue to reality. It makes the idea of God far more sensible and far more desirable.

After all, if it should be true that the nature of reality is spiritual and it is only quite temporarily and incidentally involved in matter, is it not unreasonable to want to know something of the Spiritual Being behind the Scheme of Things. And on those unimaginative people to whom the spiritual has always sounded fanciful and unreal, it is slowly dawning that the physical world which is so real and tangible to them is most uncomfortably unreliable. A man used to be able to reckon on a good number of years of active material life, which were a most efficient buffer between him and the naked spiritual realities which in his more vulnerable moments he suspected might be true. Now his buffer of material things has been shown to be far from dependable. At any moment he might be pitchforked into the world of the spirit. His anchors are slipping, and if he feels the need of anchorage (and who, at heart, does not?) he must find it in the world of the spirit—he must find God.

Beauty, Goodness, and Truth

IN ALL PROBABILITY everyone is sensitive to beauty, although obviously some are far more so than others. Yet experience shows that even those who are apparently most prosaic are touched, even to their own surprise, by certain forms of beauty. The line along which this half-melancholy, half-magic touch may come varies enormously with different people. For some it is the appealing grace of childhood, for some the surge and thunder of the sea, for some the dazzling splendor of mountain peak, for some the song of birds in spring, for some the smell of wood smoke or of frosty autumn evenings, for some—but the list is endless. All poetry and music, and art of every true sort, bear witness to man's continual falling in love with beauty, and his desperate attempt to induce beauty to live with him and enrich his common life.

The appeal of beauty which is universal, however distorted or debased it may have become, cannot be lightly dismissed. It is a pointer to something, and it certainly points to something beyond the present limitations of time and space. We can at any rate say that beauty arouses a hunger and a longing which is never satisfied (and some would say never can be satisfied) in this world.

Disabusing our minds of self-conscious righteousness, goody-goodyness, and mere absence of evil, there is something unavoidably attractive about the good. However far from the ideal our own practice may be, we have an automatic respect for such things as honesty, sincerity, faithfulness, incorruptibility, kindness, justice, and respect for other people. . . . Surely this recognition of good, so deeply rooted and so universal, is another far from negligible pointer to Reality.

Both beauty and goodness, then (no doubt in different ways), exert an effect upon man which cannot be explained in terms of the world that we know, and to this we may add his search for truth. He is not only wanting to know facts, though the careful dispassionate amassing of ascertained facts is surely one of his most admirable activities, but he also wants to find some meaning to the puzzle of life. Scientific research, philosophy, and religion, all in their different ways, attest this reaching out of man to grasp more and more truth. And yet—why should he? Why should he not rest content with what he has and what he knows? Why can he not accept death and evil and disease without worrying about them? Why does he, in all ages and in all countries, reach out to find Something—something which will harmonize and explain and complete life's bewildering phenomena? Here, too, is surely a pointer. Arguing, as we must, from what we know to what we don't know, we may fairly say that as food is the answer to hunger, water the answer to thirst, and a mate to sexual desire, this universal hunger for Truth is unlikely to be without its answer and fulfillment, however hard to find it may be.

God Focused

ALTHOUGH EVERYONE KNOWS what is meant by Beauty, Goodness, and Truth, it is impossible to visualize them as absolute values. We can visualize a beautiful thing, but not beauty; a good man, but not goodness; a true fact, but not truth. Yet once we have a beautiful thing held in our minds it is comparatively easy to fill the mind with other beauties; once we consider a truly good man we can expand and develop his qualities until we begin to get some idea of goodness; while if we are once convinced of a certain fact (particularly if we have discovered it ourselves), we can at once think of a world of truths—we begin to visualize the absolute quality of Truth.

We see beauty, then, when it is first focused for us in a beautiful thing; goodness when it is focused in a good man; truth when it is focused in a fact of which we are sure. Absolute values may exist as mental concepts for the trained philosopher; but the ordinary man must see his values focused in people or things that he knows before he can grasp them.

Let us now make a further step. The mystic claims to be able to grasp something of God in the Absolute. But the mystic is even more uncommon than the philosopher, and any attempt by the ordinary man to "imagine" God results in nothing but the "vague oblong blur" complained of by those modern people who make the attempt. Yet if a man can see God focused and be convinced that he is seeing God, scaled-down but authentic, he can, as in the case of Beauty, Truth, and Goodness, add all the other inklings and impressions that he has of the majesty, magnificence, and order of the Infinite Being, and "see God."

But can he so see God "focused"? There must be more than elusive sparks and flashes of the divine—there must be a flame burning steadily so that its light can be examined and properly assessed.

It is a fascinating problem for us human beings to consider how the Eternal Being—wishing to show men His own Character focused, His own Thought expressed, and His own Purpose demonstrated—could introduce Himself into the stream of human history without disturbing or disrupting it. There must obviously be an almost unbelievable "scaling-down" of the "size" of God to match the life of the planet. There must be a complete acceptance of the space-and-time limitations of this present life. The thing must be done properly—it must not, for example, be merely an act put on for man's benefit. If it is to be done at all God must *be* man. There could be no convincing focusing of real God in some strange semi-divine creature who enjoys supernatural advantages. Nor, though it is plain that many men have been "inspired" to utter truth, to create beauty, and to demonstrate goodness, could it suffice for a unique and authentic focusing to depend on one "super-inspired" man. For complete dependability, for universal appeal, for a personally guaranteed authenticity to which all other truth is to be related, God must do it Himself.

The Incarnation Hypothesized

SUPPOSE . . . THAT God does slip into the stream of history and is born as Baby A. A will, as far as the limitations of time, space, and circumstance allow, grow up as God "focused" in humanity, speaking a language, expressing thoughts, and demonstrating life in terms that men can understand. Having once accepted A's claim to be God expressing Himself in human terms, men will have a great deal by which to live.

First, they will know now for certain what sort of "character" the eternal God possesses. For He is certain to inform them that the man who observes Him is observing God. Secondly, the facts about man and God, the perennial anxieties about such things as pain and sin and death, the dim hopes of a more permanent world to follow this one—these and scores of other clamant questions will now have a fixed reference point, by which they can be adjusted if not settled. Thirdly, man will be able to gain at first hand information as to "what life is all about" and as to how he can co-operate with the Plan and the Power behind time and space. Fourthly, if they are convinced, as we are assuming, that the one before them is really God-become-man, they will be able to observe something absolutely unique in the history of the world: God Himself coping with life on the very terms that He has imposed upon His creatures. They will be seeing God not seated high on a throne, but down in the battlefield of life.

A, of course, having genuinely entered the space-time world and having become a human being, must enter at some particular time and must live in some particular locality. He will thus, as far as some incidentals and externals are concerned, be to some extent moulded, modified, and limited. He cannot, therefore, be a *full* expression of God— there is neither time nor space enough for that. But within the limit he sets himself he will be a perfectly genuine and adequate focusing of the nature of God. He will not only be information and example, but the aperture through which men may see more and more of God. If men are once convinced of the genuineness of his extraordinary claim, they will probably find that God is, so to speak, visible through an A-shaped aperture. Knowledge, experience, and appreciation may all expand enormously as the years pass, but that will not mean that men "grow out of" God. For A will have supplied by his demonstration in time and space one sure Fact, around which everything else of Truth, Goodness, and Beauty may be appropriately and satisfactorily crystallized.

The Hypothesis Incarnated

QUITE A NUMBER of people in all parts of the world have come to the conclusion that the hypothetical *A* has appeared in history—that *A* in fact equals the man Jesus, who was born in Palestine some nineteen centuries ago. Most of the possibilities that we have suggested might occur if God were to enter this world humanly, and historically were, they feel reasonably certain, fulfilled in the life and teaching of Jesus. And there were some remarkable additional features which could hardly have been surmised, and which we will consider in due course.

It is, of course, a very big step intellectually (and emotionally and morally as well, it will be found) to accept this famous figure of history as the designed focusing of God in human life. It is not made any easier by the clinging mass of sentimentality, superstitious reverence, and traditional associations which surround Him. It is emphatically not an easy matter for the honest modern mind to pierce the accretions and irrelevancies and see the Person, the Character— particularly as the records, though they have been examined far more closely than any other historic documents, are undeniably meager. Further, many people who have a vague childish affection for a half-remembered Jesus, have never used their adult critical faculties on the matter at all. They hardly seem to see the paramount importance of His claim to be God. Yet, if for one moment we imagine the claim to be true, the mind almost reels at its significance. It can only mean that here is Truth, here is the Character of God, the true Design for life, the authentic Yardstick of values, the reliable confirming or correcting of all gropings and inklings about Beauty, Truth, and Goodness, about this world and the next. Life can never be wholly dark or wholly futile if once the key to its meaning is in our hands.

Although an honest adult study of the available records is essential, to decide that Jesus really was the embodiment of God in a human being is not a merely intellectual decision. Our unconscious minds will sense (even if the conscious mind does not) that to accept such a unique Fact cannot but affect the whole of our life. We may with complete detachment study and form a judgment upon a *religion*, but we cannot maintain our detachment if the subject of our inquiry proves to be God Himself. This is, of course, why many otherwise honest intellectual people will construct a neat bypass around the claim of Jesus to be God. Being people of insight and imagination, they know perfectly well that once to accept such a claim as fact would mean a readjustment of their own purposes and values and affections which they may have no wish to make. To call Jesus the greatest Figure in History or the finest Moral Teacher the world has ever seen commits no one to anything. But once to allow the startled mind to accept as fact that this man is really focused-God may commit anyone to anything! There is every excuse for blundering in the dark, but in the light there is no cover from reality. It is because we strongly sense this, and not merely because we feel that the evidence is ancient and scanty, that we shrink from committing ourselves to such a far-reaching belief as that Jesus Christ was really God.

False Gods —
Resident Policeman

To many people conscience is almost all that they have by way of knowledge of God. This still small voice which makes them feel guilty and unhappy before, during, or after wrongdoing is God speaking to them. It is this which, to some extent at least, controls their conduct. It is this which impels them to shoulder the irksome duty and choose the harder path.

Now no serious advocate of a real adult religion would deny the function of conscience, or deny that its voice may at least give some inkling of the moral order that lies behind the obvious world in which we live. Yet to make conscience into God is a highly dangerous thing to do. For one thing, as we shall see in a moment, conscience is by no means an infallible guide; and for another it is extremely unlikely that we shall ever be moved to worship, love, and serve a nagging inner voice that at worst spoils our pleasure and at best keeps us rather negatively on the path of virtue.

Conscience can be so easily perverted or morbidly developed in the sensitive person, and so easily ignored and silenced by the insensitive, that it makes a very unsatisfactory god. For while it is probably true that every normal person has an embryonic moral sense by which he can distinguish right from wrong, the development, nondevelopment, or perversion of that sense is largely a question of upbringing, training, and propaganda.

As an example of the first, we may suppose a child to be

brought up by extremely strict vegetarian parents. If the child, now grown adolescent, attempts to eat meat, he will in all probability suffer an extremely bad attack of "conscience." If he is brought up to regard certain legitimate pleasures as "worldly" and reprehensible, he will similarly suffer pangs of conscience if he seeks the forbidden springs of recreation. The voice will no doubt sound like the voice of God; but it is only the voice of the early upbringing which has conditioned his moral sense.

As an example of the second influence on the moral sense, we may take a "sportsman" who has been trained from his youth that it is "wrong" to shoot a sitting bird. Should he do so, even accidentally, he will undoubtedly feel a sense of shame and wrongdoing; though to shoot a bird flying twenty yards in front of the muzzle of his gun will not produce any sense of guilt. His conscience has been artificially trained, and it is thus that "taboos" are maintained among the civilized and uncivilized alike. . . .

Many moralists, both Christian and non-Christian, have pointed out the decline in our moral sense observed in recent years. It is at least arguable that this is almost wholly due to the decline in the firsthand absorption of Christian ideals. True Christianity has never had a serious rival in the training of the moral sense which exists in ordinary people.

Yet there are many, even among professing Christians, who are made miserable by a morbidly developed conscience, which they quite wrongly consider to be the voice of God. Many a housewife overdrives herself to please some inner voice that demands perfection. The voice may be her own demands or the relics of childhood training, but it certainly is not likely to be the voice of the Power behind the Universe.

On the other hand, the middle-aged businessman who has long ago taught his conscience to come to heel may persuade himself that he is a good-living man. He may even say, with some pride, that he would never do anything against his conscience. But it is impossible to believe that the feeble voice of the half-blind thing which he calls a conscience is in any real sense the voice of God.

Surely neither the hectically overdeveloped nor the falsely-trained, nor the moribund conscience can ever be regarded as God, or even part of Him. For if it is, God can be made to appear to the sensitive an overexacting tyrant, and to the insensitive a comfortable accommodating "Voice Within" which would never interfere with a man's pleasure.

False Gods—
Tyrannical Parent

MANY PSYCHOLOGISTS ASSURE us that the trend of the whole of a man's life is largely determined by his attitude in early years toward his parents. Many normal people, with happy childhoods behind them, may scoff at this, but nevertheless the clinics and consulting-rooms of psychiatrists are thronged with those whose inner lives were distorted in early childhood by their relationship toward their parents. Quite a lot of ordinary people, who would never dream of turning to psychiatry, nevertheless have an abnormal fear of authority, or of a dominating personality of either sex, which could without much difficulty be traced back to the tyranny of a parent. Conversely there are many who would be insulted by the name "neurotic," but who nevertheless are imperfectly adjusted to life, and whose inner sense of superiority makes them difficult to work or live with. It would again not be difficult to trace in their history a childhood of spoiling and indulgence, in which the child's natural self-love was never checked or directed outward into interest in other people. The child is truly "the father of the man."

But what has this to do with an inadequate conception of God? This, that the early conception of God is almost invariably founded upon the child's idea of his father. If he is lucky enough to have a good father this is all to the good, provided of course that the conception of God grows with the rest of his personality. But if the child is afraid (or, worse still, afraid and feeling guilty because he is afraid) of his own father, the chances are that his Father in Heaven will appear to him a fearful Being. Again, if he is lucky, he will outgrow this conception, and indeed differentiate between his early "fearful" idea and his later mature conception. But many are not able to outgrow the sense of guilt and fear, and in adult years are still obsessed with it, although it has actually nothing to do with their real relationship with the living God. It is nothing more than a parental hangover. Many priests and ministers with some knowledge of psychology will have met the person abnormally afraid of God, and will have been able to recognize the psychological, rather than the religious, significance of the fear. Some of them will have had the joy of seeing the religious faith blossom out into joy and confidence, when the psychological disharmony has been analyzed and resolved. . . . It is worth observing for the sake of those who may possibly suffer from an irrational fear of, or violent revolt from, the idea of God that the root of their trouble is probably not their "sin" or their "rebelliousness," but what they felt toward their parents when they were very young.

False Gods—
Grand Old Man

SOME SUNDAY-SCHOOL children were once asked to write down their ideas as to what God was like. The answers, with few exceptions, began something like this: "God is a very old gentleman living in Heaven . . ."! Whether this story is true or not, there is no doubt that in many children's minds God is an "old" person. This is partly due, of course, to the fact that a child's superiors are always "old" to him and God must therefore be the "oldest" of all. Moreover, a child is so frequently told that he will be able to do such-and-such a thing or understand such-and-such a matter "when he is older" that it is only natural that the Source of all strength and wisdom must seem to him very old indeed. In addition to this his mind has quite probably been filled with stories of God's activities which happened "long ago." He is in consequence quite likely to feel, and even visualize, God as someone very old.

It may be argued that there is no particular harm in this. Since the child must adapt himself to an adult world there can be nothing wrong in his concept of an "old" God. But there is nevertheless a very real danger that the child will imagine this God not merely as "old," but as "old-fashioned"; and may indeed be so impressed with God's actions in "times of old" that he may fail to grasp the idea of God operating with unimpaired energy in the present and leading forward into a hopeful future.

But even if it be admitted that to visualize God as "old"

will do a child no harm, the persistence of the idea of childhood beneath the surface of the mind may well make it difficult to develop and hold an adequate idea of God in later years. In order to test whether this "old-fashioned" concept was persisting in modern young people, a simple psychological test was recently applied to a mixed group of older adolescents. They were asked to answer, without reflection, the question, "Do you think God understands radar?" In nearly every case the reply was "No," followed of course by a laugh, as the conscious mind realized the absurdity of the answer. But, simple as this test was, it was quite enough to show that *at the back of their minds* these youngsters held an idea of God quite inadequate for modern days. Subsequent discussion showed plainly that while "they had not really thought much about it," they had freely to admit that the idea of God, absorbed some years before, existed in quite a separate compartment from their modern experience, knowledge, and outlook. It was as though they were revering the memory of a Grand Old Man, who was a great power in His day, but who could not possibly be expected to keep pace with modern progress!

False Gods— Escape Artist

THE CRITICS OF the Christian religion have often contended that a religious faith is a form of psychological "escapism." A man, they say, finding the problems and demands of adult life too much for him will attempt to return to the comfort and dependence of childhood by picturing for himself a loving parent, whom he calls God. It must be admitted that there is a good deal of ammunition ready to hand for such an attack, and the first verse of a well-known and well-loved hymn provides an obvious example:

> Jesus, Lover of my soul,
> Let me to Thy bosom fly,
> While the nearer waters roll,
> While the tempest still is high:
> Hide me, O my Saviour, hide,
> Till the storm of life be past;
> Safe into thy haven guide,
> O receive my soul at last.

Here, if the words are taken at their face value, is sheer escapism, a deliberate desire to be hidden safe away until the storm and stress of life is over, and no explaining away by lovers of the hymn can alter its plain sense. It can hardly be denied that if this is true Christianity, then the charge of "escapism," of emotional immaturity and childish regression, must be frankly conceded. But although this "God of escape" is quite common, the true Christian course is set in a very different direction. No one would accuse its Founder of immaturity in insight, thought, teaching, or conduct, and the history of the Christian Church provides thousands of examples of timid half-developed personalities who have not only found in their faith what the psychologists call integration, but have coped with difficulties and dangers in a way that makes any gibe of "escapism" plainly ridiculous.

individual. Indeed if He is Infinitely High the idea of contact with an infinitesimal individual becomes laughable. *But only if we are modeling God upon what we know of man.* That is why it is contended here that what at first sight appears to be almost a superadequate idea of God is, in reality, inadequate—it is based on too tiny a foundation. Man may be made in the image of God; but it is not sufficient to conceive God as nothing more than an infinitely magnified man.

There are, for example, those who are considerably worried by the thought of God simultaneously hearing and answering the prayers and aspirations of people all over the world. That may be because their mental picture is of a harassed telephone operator answering callers at a switchboard of superhuman size. It is really better to say frankly, "I can't imagine how it can be done" (which is the literal truth), than to confuse the mind with the picture of an enlarged man performing the impossible.

All "lofty" concepts of the greatness of God need to be carefully watched lest they turn out to be mere magnifications of certain human characteristics. We may, for instance, admire the ascetic ultraspiritual type which appears to have "a mind above" food, sexual attraction, and material comfort, for example. But if in forming a picture of the Holiness of God we are simply enlarging this spirituality and asceticism to the "nth" degree we are forced to some peculiar conclusions. Thus we may find ourselves readily able to imagine God's interest in babies (for are they not "little bits of Heaven"?), yet unable to imagine His approval, let alone design, of the acts which led to their conception!

Similarly, it is natural and right, of course, that the worship we offer to God in public should be of the highest possible quality. But that must not lead us to conceive a musically "Third-Program" god who prefers the exquisite rendering of a cynical professional choir to the ragged bawling of sincere but untutored hearts.

To hold a conception of God as a mere magnified human being is to run the risk of thinking of Him as simply the Commander-in-Chief who cannot possibly spare the time to attend to the details of His subordinates' lives. Yet to have a god who is so far beyond personality and so far removed from the human context in which we alone can appreciate "values," is to have a god who is a mere bunch of perfect qualities—which means an Idea and nothing more. We need a God with the capacity to hold, so to speak, both Big and Small in His Mind at the same time. This, the Christian religion holds, is the true and satisfying conception of God revealed by Jesus Christ.

𝓕alse 𝒢ods —
The Disappointer

To SOME PEOPLE the mental image of God is a kind of blur of disappointment. "Here," they say resentfully and usually with more than a trace of self-pity, "is One whom I trusted, but He *let me down.*" The rest of their lives is consequently shadowed by this letdown. Thenceforth there can be no mention of God, Church, religion, or even parson without starting the whole process of association with its melancholy conclusion: God is a Disappointment.

Some, of course, rather enjoy this never-failing well of grievance. The years by no means dim the tragic details of the Prayer that was Unanswered or the Disaster that was Undeserved. To recall God's unfaithfulness appears to give them the same ghoulish pleasure that others find in recounting the grisly details of their "operation." Others find, of course, that a God who has Himself failed is the best possible excuse for those who do not wish to be involved in any moral effort or moral responsibility. Any suggestion of obeying or following God can be more than countered by another glance at the perennial Grievance. . . .

The people who feel that God is a Disappointment have not understood the terms on which we inhabit this planet. They are wanting a world in which good is rewarded and evil is punished—as in a well-run kindergarten. They want to see the good man prosper invariably, and the evil man suffer invariably, here and now. There is, of course, nothing wrong with their sense of justice. But they misunderstand the conditions of this present temporary life in which God withholds His Hand, in order, so to speak, to allow room for His plan of free will to work itself out. Justice will be fully vindicated when the curtain falls on the present stage, the houselights go on, and we go out into the Real World.

There will always be times when from our present limited point of view we cannot see the wood for the trees. Glaring injustice and pointless tragedy will sometimes be quite beyond our control and our understanding. We can, of course, postulate an imaginary God with less good sense, love, and justice than we have ourselves; and we may find a perverse pleasure in blaming Him. But that road leads nowhere. You cannot worship a Disappointment.

False Gods—
Narcissus on the Silver Screen

JUST AS THE cinema apparatus projects onto the screen a large image from a picture about the size of a postage stamp, so the human mind has a tendency to "project" onto other people ideas and emotions that really exist in itself. The guilty man, for example, will project onto other people suspicion and disapproval, even though they are completely ignorant of his guilt. This, of course, is an everyday psychological phenomenon.

We tend to do the same thing in our mental conception of God. . . . A harsh and puritanical society will project its dominant qualities and probably postulate a hard and puritanical god. A lax and easygoing society will probably produce a god with about as much moral authority as Father Christmas.

The same tendency is observable in individual cases. We have already noted . . . how a certain type of keen Churchman, for example, tends to produce a god of Impeccable Churchmanship. But, of course, the inclination goes farther than this, and there is always a danger of imagining a god with moral qualities like our own, vastly magnified and purified of course, and *with the same blind spots*. Thus the god whom we imagine may have his face set against drunkenness (an evil which, though it does not tempt us, fills us with horror and indignation), may turn a blind eye to our business methods because he feels, as we do, that "business is business"!

Obviously, unless the conception of God is something higher than a Magnification of our own Good Qualities, our service and worship will be no more and no less than the service and worship of ourselves. Such a god may be a prop to our self-esteem but is, naturally, incapable of assisting us to win a moral victory and will be found in time of serious need to fade disconcertingly away.

Moreover, we are so made that we cannot really be satisfied with a mere projection. Even Narcissus must at times have grown tired of admiring his own reflection! The very fact that in choosing a friend or a life-partner men frequently choose someone very different from themselves is enough to show that they are not only and forever seeking an echo of their own personalities. If we are to be moved to real worship and stirred to give of ourselves, it must be by Something not merely infinitely higher but Something "other" than ourselves. . . .

The god who is wholly, or even partially, a mere projection of ourselves is quite inadequate for life's demands and can never arouse in us true worship or service. Indeed he is as real a danger as the pool became at last to Narcissus.

False Gods—
Olympic Sprinter

IF THERE IS one thing which should be quite plain to those who accept the revelation of God in Nature and the Bible it is that He is never in a hurry. Long preparation, careful planning, and slow growth would seem to be leading characteristics of spiritual life. Yet there are many people whose religious tempo is feverish. With a fine disregard for its context they flourish like a banner the text, "The King's business requireth haste," and proceed to drive themselves and their followers nearly mad with tension and anxiety! "Consider," cries the passionate advocate of foreign missions, "that every second, thousands of pagan souls pass into a Christless eternity." "Evangelize to a finish in this generation!" cries the enthusiastic young convert at his missionary meeting.

It is refreshing, and salutary, to study the poise and quietness of Christ. His task and responsibility might well have driven a man out of his mind. But He was never in a hurry, never impressed by numbers, never a slave of the clock. He was acting, He said, as He observed God to act—never in a hurry.

False Gods— Mystical Vision

IT IS CHARACTERISTIC of human beings to create and revere a "privileged class," and some modern Christians regard the mystic as being somehow spiritually a cut above his fellows. Ordinary forms of worship and prayer may suffice for the ordinary man, but for the one who has direct apprehension of God—he is literally in a class by himself. You cannot expect a man to attend Evensong in his parish church when there are visions waiting for him in his study!

The New Testament does not subscribe to this flattering view of those with a gift for mystic vision. It is always downright and practical. It is by their fruits that men shall be known: God is no respecter of persons: true religion is expressed by such humdrum things as visiting those in trouble and steadfastly maintaining faith despite exterior circumstances. It is not, of course, that the New Testament considers it a bad thing for a man to have a vision of God, but there is a wholesome insistence on such a vision being worked out in love and service.

It should be noted, at least by those who accept Christ's claim to be God, that He by no means fits into the picture of the "mystic saint." Those who are fascinated by the supposed superiority of the mystic soul might profitably compile a list of its characteristics and place them side by side with those of Christ. The result would probably expose a surprising conclusion.

There is, in fact, no provision for a "privileged class" in genuine Christianity. "It shall not be so among you," said Christ to His early followers, "all ye are brethren."

False Gods—the Ultimate Bundle of Highest Values

THIS CONCEPTION IS one of the most "enlightened" and "modern." God is completely depersonalized and becomes the Ultimate Bundle of Highest Values. Such an idea is usually held by those who lead sheltered lives and who have little experience of the crude stuff of ordinary human life. It is manifestly impossible for any except the most intellectual to hold in his mind (let alone worship and serve) a God who is no more than what we think to be the highest values raised to the "nth" degree.

False Gods—
Idol of the Worshipping Animal

MAN HAS RIGHTLY been defined as a "worshipping animal." If for some reason he has no God, he will unquestionably worship *something*. Common modern substitutes are the following: the State, success, efficiency, money, "glamor," power, even security. Nobody, of course, calls them "God"; but they have the influence and command the devotion which should belong to the real God. It is only when a man finds God that he is able to see how his worshipping instinct has been distorted and misdirected.

Four Prophets

I CHOSE THESE PROPHETS, Amos, Hosea, Isaiah, and Micah, partly because the period of their ministry was such a crucial time in the history of God's chosen people; and partly because they pierce through a great many falsities (including religious falsities). Time and again they touch the very heart of the matter—the way in which men behave toward each other and the way in which they worship God; and all of these prophets can see that those two things are inseparable. They are thus, as it were, clearing the ground for the revolutionary teaching that was to come with the Gospel of Jesus Christ.

The people of Israel had never been so affluent as they were when Amos attempted rudely to awaken them. But with prosperity had come inhumanity to man—"the rich got rich and the poor got poorer"—and the worship of the false gods of riches, success, and security. Moral values had slumped and even common honesty and decent neighborliness were being squeezed out by greed and corruption. These four prophets could clearly see this galloping spiritual deterioration, and they not only denounced it but declared in no uncertain terms the consequences of moral and social evil. As prophets they "saw the truth," and as prophets they were constrained to declare what they saw. They were not necessarily foretelling the future, although history proves what remarkably accurate prophets they were in that sense, but they had to warn, even in the most terrifying terms, a people grown deaf and blind to the truth.

All of these prophetic books include what we might call, if we only read superficially, "a happy ending." But this is because the prophets could see far ahead. As in the "apocalyptic" passages in the synoptic Gospels, or in the Revelation of St. John the Divine, the earthly time-sense is in abeyance. Immediate future and far distant future are equally in focus. I do not myself see any cogent reason for supposing that these visions of a later people returning purified to their own land must be the work "of a later hand." If these prophets could see, with remarkable accuracy, what lay a few years ahead, why not a few hundred or a few thousand years?

But despite their visions, or, if we think more deeply, perhaps because of them, these proclaimers of the truth are solidly down to earth. They will not permit religion to exist in a vacuum. Unless man's worship of God is matched by his just and fair treatment of his neighbor, then ceremonies, rituals, observances, and sacrifices are nauseating to God. And they are highly dangerous to the worshipper because he is attempting to stifle his moral and social conscience by all the "business" of religion. He is, in fact, attempting to bribe God. This is what moves all of these prophets, in their different ways, to such violent indignation.

This declaration of the indissoluble connection between the way in which we love God and the way in which we love our neighbor seems to me unique in the religions of the ancient world. Many religions, though not all, have taught mankind to be merciful and charitable, but the Hebrew prophets are, I believe, alone in declaring the uses of religion to be entirely null and void unless men are treating their fellow men with mercy and justice. To a prophet of the caliber of these men it is not enough to drop a coin into the beggar's palm; you must ask yourself, *"How far am I responsible for his being a beggar at all?"* And this is a thoroughly relevant question today.

This marriage of the love of God and the love of man was the backbone of Christ's teaching seven hundred years later. Sometimes I think we forget that he taught quite categorically that we cannot be forgiven by God unless we also forgive those who injure or offend us. And perhaps not enough notice is taken of the only picture Christ ever painted of the Last Judgment, recorded in the twenty-fifth chapter of St. Matthew's Gospel. Here it is most plainly stated that the way we treat our fellows is an exact replica of the way in which we are treating the Son of God himself— surely a piercing and devastating truth if ever there was one! I am myself not overblessed with a historical sense, but I am amazed that these bold men were declaring such vital truth in the days of Homer, long before the heyday of Athens, and when Rome, the so-called "eternal city," was little more than a village.

Despite the distance in time, the frequent unfamiliarity of

idiom and the imperfect state of the Hebrew text, these four men speak with uncommon authority. All four strongly convey the sense that they are seeing the truth about God and man. There is something peculiarly compelling about men who have the deepest possible reverence for God and yet can say, "This is what the Lord says."

In these books there are some crude anthropomorphisms which offend our modern minds, and, naturally, the conception of God is a pre-Christian one. Nevertheless we are left with an overwhelming conviction that God is God, right is right, and wrong is wrong; and that in itself is an iron tonic to us moderns. For most of us today are afraid of denouncing evil for fear of being called intolerant; we are not allowed to be morally indignant for "psychology says" that what is making us angry is an identical fault in ourselves! We are not allowed to have any definite values of right and wrong, for all things, we are told, are purely relative— though relative to *what* is not made clear. In these days we can scarcely spare a thought for the victim of vicious assault, for all our sympathy is needed for the brutal and callous aggressor. We are frightened of sharing our faith with a fellow human being for fear of interfering with the sanctity of his private beliefs; we are even scared of living out the principles of the Gospel lest we are labeled contemptuously as "do-gooders."

But here in this world of nearly three thousand years ago human beings are far less self-conscious. They can be noble, wise, brave, and good, but they can also be cruel, stupid, greedy, fickle, or just plain wicked. We are back in a world of real people, potentially sons and daughters of the Most High, but making tragically wrong choices and treating each other abominably. But these four prophets assume always that men have consciences and that they have the power to choose their path. If they are beyond the reach of messages of sweetness and light, then violent, indeed terrifying, threats and warnings must be used to crack their dreadful complacency.

These men were not in the least concerned to make their message "acceptable." They were not out to placate the people in power or to conciliate the clever; their whole purpose was to speak "the word of the Lord." Such voices of integrity, despite all the obscurities and difficulties of the text, still sound like a trumpet down the centuries.

It seems to me (and Heaven knows any honest man can observe this in his own spirit) that human beings are forever trying to evade moral responsibility, while God is eternally trying to make them accept it, and thus grow up into being His sons. Because of this human tendency the world of the Bible is bound to be an uncomfortable world. For here God, not man, is master. Here God speaks and man, if he is wise, will listen with a proper humility.

The Visited Planet

ONCE UPON A TIME a very young angel was being shown round the splendors and glories of the universes by a senior and experienced angel. To tell the truth, the little angel was beginning to be tired and a little bored. He had been shown whirling galaxies and blazing suns, infinite distances in the deathly cold of interstellar space, and to his mind there seemed to be an awful lot of it all. Finally he was shown the galaxy of which our planetary system is but a small part. As the two of them drew near to the star which we call our sun and to its circling planets, the senior angel pointed to a small and rather insignificant sphere turning very slowly on its axis. It looked as dull as a dirty tennis ball to the little angel whose mind was filled with the size and glory of what he had seen.

"I want you to watch that one particularly," said the senior angel, pointing with his finger.

"Well, it looks very small and rather dirty to me," said the little angel. "What's special about that one?"

"That," replied his senior solemnly, "is the Visited Planet."

" 'Visited'?" said the little one. "You don't mean visited by—"

"Indeed I do. That ball, which I have no doubt looks to you small and insignificant and perhaps not overclean, has been visited by our young Prince of Glory." And at these words he bowed his head reverently.

"But how?" queried the younger one. "Do you mean that our great and glorious Prince, with all these wonders and splendors of His Creation, and millions more that I'm sure I haven't seen yet, went down in Person to this fifth-rate little ball? Why should He do a thing like that?"

"It isn't for us," said his senior, a little stiffly, "to question His 'why's,' except that I must point out to you that He is not impressed by size and numbers as you seem to be. But that He really went I know, and all of us in Heaven who know anything know that. As to why He became one of them . . . how else do you suppose could He visit them?"

The little angel's face wrinkled in disgust.

"Do you mean to tell me," he said, "that He stooped so low as to become one of those creeping, crawling creatures of that floating ball?"

"I do, and I don't think He would like you to call them 'creeping crawling creatures' in that tone of voice. For, strange as it may seem to us, He loves them. He went down to visit them to lift them up to become like Him."

The little angel looked blank. Such a thought was almost beyond his comprehension.

"Close your eyes for a moment," said the senior angel, "and we will go back in what they call Time."

While the little angel's eyes were closed and the two of them moved nearer to the spinning ball, it stopped its spinning, spun backward quite fast for a while, and then slowly resumed its usual rotation.

"Now look!" and as the little angel did as he was told, there appeared here and there on the dull surface of the globe little flashes of light, some merely momentary and some persisting for quite a time.

"Well, what am I seeing now?" queries the little angel.

"You are watching this little world as it was some thousands of years ago," returned his companion. "Every flash and glow of light that you see is something of the Father's knowledge and wisdom breaking into the minds and hearts of people who live upon the earth. Not many people, you see, can hear His Voice or understand what He says, even though He is speaking gently and quietly to them all the time."

"Why are they so blind and deaf and stupid?" asked the junior angel rather crossly.

"It is not for us to judge them. We who live in the Splendor have no idea what it is like to live in the dark. We hear the music and the Voice like the sound of many waters every day of our lives, but to them—well, there is much darkness and much noise and much distraction upon the earth. Only a few who are quiet and humble and wise hear His Voice. But watch, for in a moment you will see something truly wonderful."

The Earth went on turning and circling round the sun, and then, quite suddenly, in the upper half of the globe there appeared a light, tiny, but so bright in its intensity that both the angels hid their eyes.

"I think I can guess," said the little angel in a low voice. "That was the Visit, wasn't it?"

"Yes, that was the Visit. The Light Himself went down there and lived among them; but in a moment, and you will be able to tell that even with your eyes closed, the light will go out."

"But why? Could He not bear their darkness and stupidity? Did He have to return here?"

"No, it wasn't that," returned the senior angel. His voice was stern and sad. "They failed to recognize Him for Who He was—or at least only a handful knew Him. For the most part they preferred their darkness to His Light, and in the end they killed Him."

"The fools, the crazy fools! They don't deserve—"

"Neither you nor I nor any other angel knows why they were so foolish and so wicked. Nor can we say what they deserve or don't deserve. But the fact remains, they killed our Prince of Glory while He was Man amongst them."

"And that, I suppose, was the end? I see the whole Earth has gone black and dark. All right, I won't judge them, but surely that is all they could expect?"

"Wait. We are still far from the end of the story of the Visited Planet. Watch now, but be ready to cover your eyes again."

In utter blackness the Earth turned round three times, and then there blazed with unbearable radiance a point of light.

"What now?" asked the little angel, shielding his eyes.

"They killed Him, all right, but He conquered death. The thing most of them dread and fear all their lives He broke and conquered. He rose again, and a few of them saw Him, and from then on became His utterly devoted slaves."

"Thank God for that!" said the little angel.

"Amen. Open your eyes now; the dazzling light has gone. The Prince has returned to His Home of Light. But watch the Earth now."

As they looked, in place of the dazzling light there was a

bright glow which throbbed and pulsated. And then as the Earth turned many times, little points of light spread out. A few flickered and died, but for the most part the lights burned steadily, and as they continued to watch, in many parts of the globe there was a glow over many areas.

"You see what is happening?" asked the senior angel. "The bright glow is the company of loyal men and women He left behind, and with His help they spread the glow, and now lights begin to shine all over the Earth."

"Yes, yes," said the little angel impatiently. "But how does it end? Will the little lights join up with one another? Will it all be light, as it is in Heaven?"

His senior shook his head. "We simply don't know," he replied. "It is in the Father's hands. Sometimes it is agony to watch, and sometimes it is joy unspeakable. The end is not yet. But now I am sure you can see why this little ball is so important. He has visited it; He is working out His Plan upon it."

"Yes, I see, though I don't understand. I shall never forget that this is the Visited Planet. . . ."

Jesus' Strength as a Man

WHAT HAPPENED TO me as [my translation of the Gospels] progressed was that the figure of Jesus emerged more and more clearly, and in a way unexpectedly. Of course I had a deep respect, indeed a great reverence, for the conventional Jesus Christ whom the Church worshipped. But I was not at all prepared for the *unconventional* man revealed in those terse Gospels. No one could possibly have invented such a person: this was no puppet-hero built out of the imaginations of adoring admirers. "This man Jesus," so briefly described, rang true, sometimes alarmingly true. I began to see now why the religious establishment of those days wanted to get rid of him at all costs. He was sudden death to pride, pomposity, and pretence.

This man could be moved with compassion and could be very gentle, but I could find no trace of the "Gentle Jesus, meek and mild." He was quite terrifyingly tough, not in a Bulldog Drummond-James Bond sort of way, but by the sheer strength of a unified and utterly dedicated personality. He once (at least) walked unscathed through a murderous crowd. I have known a few—a very, very few—men who could do that. But then I find that this sheer strength was still his after hours of unspeakable agony in the garden of Gethsemane. Those who were sent to arrest him "fell back to the ground." Previous pious generations attribute this to some supernatural power. I do not believe this for a moment. Jesus was a man of such complete authority that he could remain in command of a situation even when the odds were heavily against him.

It was this strength of human character which struck me again and again. We are not being told of a superman but of someone supremely human. He could work so hard that his followers begged him to stop. Yet he was fast asleep aboard the little fishing boat while the others did the rowing. He was awake and out praying in solitude while the others were asleep, yet there were times when he was tired. "Jesus, being wearied with his journey, sat down beside a well," records John. He touched the untouchable leper, he made friends with those who had lost their reputation and self-respect. He denounced in vitriolic words the leaders of so-called religion. He spoke fearlessly to the violently insane. He wept in the presence of human sorrow. He also wept over Jerusalem because its people utterly failed to recognize God's Messiah when he taught and preached among them, and also because, with the true prophet's insight, he foresaw the city's hideous destruction. With even a little imaginative sympathy one could sense the agony of his frustration and near-despair. For the first time it seemed to me that it was because he was a human being almost at the end of his tether that this man cursed a fig tree and then in the garden called for swords instead of cloaks. He admitted that he was terrified as he went into the garden of Gethsemane, and he sweated there in fear and anguish.

The record of the behavior of Jesus on the way to the Cross and of the Crucifixion itself is almost unbearable, chiefly because it is so intensely *human*. If, as I believe, this was indeed God focused in a human being, we can see for ourselves that here is no play acting, this is the real thing. There are no supernatural advantages for this man. No celestial rescue party delivered him from the power of evil men, and his agony was not mitigated by any superhuman anesthetic. We can only guess what frightful anguish of mind and spirit wrung from him the terrible words, "My God, my God, why hast thou forsaken me?" But the cry "It is finished!" cannot be one of despair. It does not even mean, "It is all over." It means, "It has been completed"— and the terrifying task of doing God's will to the bitter end had been fully and finally accomplished.

Here, in the four Gospels, fragmentary as they sometimes are, emerges a real man, whose perfect integrity is compelling. He "spoke with authority," and "the common people heard him gladly," and even at the end of his public career, those who were sent to arrest him returned empty handed. "Never man spake like this man," was their comment.

But it would be a profound mistake to think that Jesus was merely an eloquent field preacher who had got on the wrong side of authority. His character was strange and unpredictable. He was meek in the way that only the strong can truly be, yet he called, demanded, and commanded without explanation or apology. What other man could call some fishermen to leave their skilled jobs or ask somebody else to give up the lucrative, even though despised, work of tax collecting and to follow him, and succeed? What other man could look straight at a ring of hostile faces and throw out the challenge, "Which of you convinces me of sin?" and yet give no impression of arrogance or self-righteousness?

Yet the flashes of light upon this character which the four Gospels reveal are often surprising. Jesus was not some penniless ascetic like John the Baptist before him. Luke records that there were many women who "ministered to him of their substance." We may be pretty sure that the house of Mary and Martha was not the only home where he could find rest and refreshment. His cloak, "woven without seam," was hardly the covering of a beggar. There can be no doubt that he was socially popular, and although we can discount the jibe that he was "a gluttonous man and a wine bibber," we can fairly infer that he enjoyed God's good gifts of food and wine.

It struck me again and again that some of the unexpected sayings and actions of Jesus were recorded just because they were unexpected. The routine work (if we might so describe it) is sometimes dismissed in a few words—"he went about doing good and healing all manner of sickness and disease among the people." But the other words and works, which no one could have anticipated, and which must have been nearly inexplicable at the time, are trea- sured and remembered with the utmost fidelity.

Yet woe betide any man who tries to fit this man into any political or humanitarian slot! Those pacifists who would claim him as their champion would do well to remember that it was a soldier, a Roman commissioned officer, who most evoked the admiration of Jesus. The parable of the tal- ents is enough to show that Jesus recognized the fundamen- tal *inequality* of men in ability and possessions. The stories

of Jesus abound in such inequalities, in the difference between master and man, hard working and lazy, prudent
and improvident. It is true that he denounced hypocrisy,
exploitation, and lack of compassion. But he made no attempt, as probably Judas Iscariot hoped, to make himself a
national champion. The "other-worldly" aspect of his teaching cannot be fairly ignored. "My kingdom," he insisted,
"is not of this world." Yet it had already "come upon men
unawares" and was even then "among" or "within" them.
The way men treated one another in this world was of paramount importance, but Jesus recognized the obvious un-
fairness and injustice in the here-and-now. In the end, justice would be done and be seen to be done, but not in this
time-and-space world. Jesus was no sentimental "do-
gooder," and he spoke quite unequivocally about rewards
and punishments "in the world to come." He declared that
a man who harmed one of his "little ones" would be better
off dead. Some of the most terrifying words ever written in
the New Testament are put into the mouth of Jesus. Yet
they are not threats or menaces but warnings given in
deadly earnest by the incarnation of unsentimental love.

What I am concerned with here is not to write a new life
of Jesus, but to set down my witness to the continued
shocks which his words and deeds gave me as I approached
the Gospels uninsulated by the familiar cover of beautiful
language. The figure who emerged is quite unlike the Jesus
of conventional piety, and even more unlike that imagined
hero whom members of various causes claim as their champion. What we are so often confronted with today is a "processed" Jesus. Every element that we feel is not consonant
with our "image" of him is removed, and the result is more
insipid and unsatisfying than the worst of processed food.

Jesus' Miracles

IN THE PROCESS of translation, a definite and indeed authoritative human character emerged from the combined writings of the Evangelists. This man Jesus was much more of a human being than I had previously thought. I suppose that somewhere in the recesses of my mind I had stored a mixed-up impression of a being of supernatural perfection and certain supernatural powers. I believed, and indeed still do believe, that Jesus was both God and man. But the conclusion grew upon me that the Jesus of the Gospels really *was* man, not a demigod and certainly not God playing, however convincingly, the part of man. I have written of the mental and spiritual toughness which coexisted in Jesus with extraordinary sympathy and compassion. So that when I came to the "miracles" of the Gospels I did not find in them anything incompatible with his character or his declared mission. They did not give me the impression of being celestial conjuring tricks designed to produce faith. Indeed the records insist that Jesus did not want publicity for his acts of physical or mental healing. I think it is difficult for us today to appreciate the spiritual power of a man uniquely integrated and dedicated, and who spent many hours in solitary communion with God. The sense grew upon me with the years that such a man, so toughened and disciplined in following the path laid out for him by his Father, might quite easily possess qualities of insight into the cause of a man's sickness, as well as the power to make him whole. Again, we need not quarrel with the picture language. To those who saw the outward manifestations of an epileptic or some mental disorder which made a man violently destructive, it was not unnatural to think of him as possessing or being possessed by "a devil." Indeed those of us who have ever been in the presence of the violently deranged and looked into their eyes could easily agree that some evil power appears to be possessing the patient. It seems that Jesus was in many cases able to get to the storm center of the disturbance and resolve it with authoritative love. We do not know even yet how far the mind affects the body or the body the mind, or how far either of them are influenced by spiritual power—by intercessory prayer, for example. We know how to "cure" certain diseases with fair accuracy, but what we are really doing is removing the obstacles which are preventing a natural ability to heal itself which both the human body and mind possess. It does not seem to me in the least unreasonable that a man of concentrated spiritual power should be able to remove these obstacles instantaneously. The whole business of "spiritual" healing is a much debated one, and I do not propose to enter any controversy here. I am simply concerned to record my own conviction that the miracles of healing which Jesus performed were perfectly genuine, even though they may be described in the jargon of the day.

This brings me to another important point. What we read in the Gospels is, I believe, true, but it is not necessarily described in words which we should use today, nearly two thousand years afterwards. A simple example springs to mind. In the three hours of darkness which fell over the whole countryside at the crucifixion of Jesus, Luke says that the sun's light failed, using the very Greek word which we use when we talk about an eclipse. Luke gives me the impression of being a very careful writer who, to use our modern phrase, would "interview" people about what they remembered of the life and teaching of Jesus. Now *we* know that there could not have been an eclipse of the sun, because that cannot happen at the time of the full moon, which was when Jesus died. We do not know whether Luke himself knew this. But since he records the failure of the sun's light and goes on to describe the dismay and confusion it caused (for men had no means of telling that the unnatural event was to last no more than three hours), it is perfectly possible that an eyewitness of that eerie darkness at noon might well have described it to Luke as an eclipse of the sun. We may never know in this life the cause of the phenomenon, but I believe that it happened, and as a Christian I believe it to be a singularly impressive reflection in the natural world of what was happening on the Cross.

To me this applies to any of the "miracles" of Jesus. Whether we one day know the laws of the spiritual sphere in which he was moving or not, I believe that the Evangelists were setting down in terms of their own time what they actually observed. I am not therefore particularly worried when Mark reports that at the baptism of Jesus he (Jesus), "saw the heavens split open, and the Spirit coming down upon him like a dove. A voice came out of Heaven, saying, 'You are my dearly beloved Son, in whom I am well pleased!' " (Mark 1:10–11). Whether Jesus alone saw this sight and heard these words, and later told his disciples about the occurrence, or whether there were those of sufficient spiritual perception to see and hear what happened, I do not know. For myself, I believe it happened, but whether I should have heard any voice or seen anything beyond a flash of light is naturally open to question. It is very interesting to find that in John's Gospel, where a "voice from heaven" speaks to Jesus shortly before his suffering and death, John records, "When the crowd of bystanders heard this, they said it thundered, but some of them said, 'An angel spoke to him' " (John 12:29). What then, I am concerned about is my conviction that many extraordinary events accompanied the life of Jesus, but they are necessarily described in the language of those who were eyewitnesses.

There is a good deal in the New Testament about light and darkness, and I think we should constantly remind ourselves to what an extent we take artificial light for granted. Most of us live within touch of an electric light switch, many of us live in cities and towns whose streets and houses are illuminated, and the electric torch operated by a battery is a commonplace almost all over the world. But in the world of the first century A.D. light created a much greater impression of divine presence or divine happening than speed or size or physical power, which are the things which impress many of us today. The story of the Transfiguration is a particularly good example of this. The dazzling brightness of both the face of Jesus and his clothes filled Peter, James, and John with exalted awe. I find this story interesting for another reason. Peter, James, and John described what they saw, and they observed Moses and Elijah talking to Jesus. It seems to me it would be quite possible to relate the incident in a different way. Suppose that the limitations of time and earthly life were, so to speak, momentarily fixed. Peter, James, and John would then see Jesus radiantly bright, talking without the sightest sense of anachronism with the two men of the past who represented the Law and the prophets. Thus one could say not so much that Jesus was transfigured but that the disciples were temporary relieved of their earth-blindness. It must have been an ecstatic experience and one which Peter, quite understandably, but in a rather clumsy way, wanted to prolong. Once again, to me it bears the hallmark of a true happening, however shortly and naively described.

Jesus' Prophecy

CLOSELY ALLIED TO the miraculous elements in the life of
Jesus is the authentic note of prophecy. Most people who
know the Bible at all know that prophecy does not necessarily mean foretelling the future, although it may well include
it. I have so far only made one excursion into the world of
the Old Testament [*Four Prophets*] but a close study of the
prophets' message shows that such men are primarily concerned to declare the "Word of the Lord." They saw, sometimes with startling and heartbreaking clarity, what would
be bound to happen if the nation continued on a course
contrary to the will of the Lord. The time sense was temporarily suspended, there is a dramatic "foreshortening" of
things which were to come. More frequently than not, their
vision was astonishingly accurate, even though twenty or a
hundred years might elapse before what they foresaw came
true. Their messages were "early warnings" rather than
long-term threats. Prophecy is not necessarily prediction.
For the warning contained in the vision might lead to a
change of heart, and therefore of subsequent events.

I found this same prophetic note in the teaching of Jesus
as recorded by the first three Evangelists. At first I was
tempted to think that various warnings of persecution and
trouble in the future made by Jesus at different times had
been put by some first-century Christian Jew into the accepted apocalyptic form. Certainly there is a marked change
of key; Jesus is not now giving definite teaching or even
speaking in parables; he is speaking as the prophets spoke.
He was, of course, on intimate terms with the prophetic

writings of the Old Testament, and he must have known the special form in which much of that prophecy is set. So I came to change my view, and I believe now that there were times when Jesus, probably to the inner circle of the disciples, shared his insights about the future in the prophetic idiom which they would to some extent understand. He knew that terrible persecutions would follow his death, he could foresee the wars and famines, the terrible sufferings which were to befall humanity. He could see "men's hearts failing them for fear" as they saw the inevitable approach of terrible destruction. He also spoke of his own "coming" as being as unexpected as a thief in the night but as unmistakably conspicuous as a flash of lightning. He spoke of himself as "coming" to judge the world. He wondered whether there would still be "faith" in the world when he should finally come. He knew how men's faith in God can be eroded by the anxieties and the many apparent injustices as well as by the present prosperity of evil. "Because iniquity shall abound, the love of many shall wax cold" (Matthew 24:12).

What Jesus Says About the Character of God

WHAT SORT OF person is God? Christ's answer is quite unequivocal. He is "the Father." When we hear this familiar truth we nearly always read back into God's Character what we know of fatherhood. This is understandable enough, but it reverses the actual truth. If God is "the Father," in Nature and Character and Operation, then we derive (if we are parents) our characteristics from Him. We are reproducing, no doubt on a microscopic scale and in a thoroughly faulty manner, something of the Character of God. If once we accept it as true that the whole Power behind this astonishing Universe is of that kind of character that Christ could only describe as "Father," the whole of life is transfigured. If we are really seeing in human relationships fragmentary and faulty but real reflections of the Nature of God, a flood of light is immediately released upon all the life that we can see. People and our relationships with them at once become of tremendous importance. Much of life is seen to be merely its setting, its stage, its "props"—the *business* of it is in the realm of personality; it is people not things that matter. It is thus quite impossible to divorce Christianity from life. Those who attempted to divorce the religion of their day from ordinary life were called by Christ, "play-actors" (hypocrites), i.e., they were acting a part and not really living at all.

What Jesus Says About the Purpose of Life

WHAT IS THE purpose of life? Christ did not give an answer to this question in its modern cynical form which implies, "Is it worth living at all?"; but He did answer those who wanted to know what to do with the vitality, affections, and talents with which they were endowed. He also answered those who already saw intuitively that this present life was transitory and incomplete and wanted to know how to be incorporated into the main timeless Stream of Life itself. The questions are really much the same. In both cases men wanted to know how they could be at one with Life's real purpose. And of course they still do. He said that there were really two main principles of living on which all true morality and wisdom might be said to depend. The first was to love God with the whole of a man's personality, and the second to love his fellow men as much and in the same way as he naturally loved himself. If these two principles were obeyed Christ said that a man would be in harmony with the Purpose of Life, which transcends time.

These two principles, one of which deals with the Invisible and Unchanging, the other with the visible and variable, cover the total relationships of a man's life. Christ made them intensely practical and indissolubly connected. The expression of love for God did not lie in formal piety nor in mystical contemplation, but in obedience to what He believed to be the will of God, which very often meant, in fact, the succoring and service of other men. A man could not be "friends with" God on any other terms than complete obedience to Him, and that included being "friends with" his fellow men. Christ stated emphatically that it was quite impossible in the nature of things for a man to be at peace with God and at variance with his neighbor. This disquieting fact is often hushed up, but it is undeniable that Christ said it, and the truth of it is enshrined (or should we say more properly embalmed) in the petition for forgiveness in the all-too-familiar "Lord's Prayer."

The Purpose of Life would seem to be the gradual winning of men to a willing loyalty to these two principles, the establishing of the Rule of God. Christ labeled the first one "primary and most important," probably because unless principles and values are first established by loving the true God there will not be "enough love to go round." The world would go on loving its own selected circle, despising, exploiting, or hating those outside it unless their hearts were first attuned to "the Father." Those who have exalted the second principle to the neglect of the first have again and again proved the wisdom of Christ's choice of their order.

What Jesus Says About Pride, Self-Righteousness, and the Exploitation of Others

WHAT IS REALLY wrong with the world? This is an extremely important question if only because it is asked so often and answered in so many different ways. Christ answered it, not directly, but quite plainly by implication. It is here, in diagnosis, that it is perhaps most important of all to realize the paramount authority of what Christ said. None of us thinks or speaks or feels without bias, and all of us are prone to fit facts to a theory. Christ had no bias and no theory: He came to give us the facts, and they are quite plainly, that this "power-to-love" which He recommended should be expended on God and other people, has been turned in on itself. The basic problems of happiness are not intellectual, but emotional. It is "out of the heart," according to Christ, that there proceed all those things which spoil relationships whether between individuals or between groups of people.

It is obvious, if we accept Christ's two great principles, that "sin" will lie in the refusal to follow them. To Christ the most serious sin was not the misdirection of the love-energy, which might be due to ignorance or mere carelessness, but the deliberate refusal to allow it to flow out either to God or to other people. This accounts for some of His

tion. The narrow road of following the basic rules which, because it is in harmony with God, is not affected by what we call death, was being followed by comparatively few. His plan of rescue (or salvation, to use a much misused word) had to begin with a tiny minority. They were to be the spearhead of good against evil.

2. Christ definitely spoke of a power of spiritual evil, and, using the language of His contemporaries, He called this power "Satan," "the Devil," or "the Evil One." Now whatever mystery lies behind the existence of such an evil spiritual power—whether we accept a Miltonic idea of a fallen angelic power or whether we conceive the evil spirit in the world as arising out of the cumulative effects of centuries of selfish living—there can be no blinking the fact that Christ spoke, and acted, on the assumption that there is a power of evil operating in the world. If we accept as fact His claim to be God this must make us think seriously.

We are so accustomed by modern thought to regard evil as "error," as the "growing pains" of civilization, or simply as an inexplicable problem, that once more the mind does not readily accept what is in effect God's own explanation—that there is a spirit of evil operating in the world. We find Christ speaking quite plainly of this spirit as responsible for disease and insanity as well as being the unremitting enemy of those who want to follow the new, true order.

Modern man has a lust for full explanation and habitually considers himself in no way morally bound unless he is in full possession of all the facts. Hence, of course, the prevalence of noncommittal agnosticism. Yet it would seem that Christ, God-become Man, did not give men a full explanation of the origin and operation of the evil forces in this world. (It is perfectly possible that in our present space-time existence we could not comprehend it, anyway.) But He did recognize evil as evil, not as a mere absence of good: He did, wherever He found it possible, destroy evil. He did indicate the lines along which evil could be defeated and He did talk of the positive resources which would be necessary for such defeat, and these we must consider a little later.

The Good Shepherd

IN ST. JOHN 10 our Lord contrasts Himself as the Good Shepherd in whose care the sheep find food and security, with the thieves and robbers who came before Him. I have often wondered whom He had in mind, for the words as they stand, "All that came before me are thieves and robbers" (St. John 10:8) sound rather harsh. It is probable that in the contemporary situation Christ had in mind leaders of men, political, national, and even religious, who really, in the long run, destroyed or sold for their own ends the souls of men. There are many "thieves and robbers" in the situation today who are similarly exploiting and destroying personality. We think of the soul-destroying aims and methods of Communism, of false religions which ask so much of men and in the end give them nothing. We think of the blight of materialism which by flattering a man's importance in this life deprives him of his destiny as a son of God. We think of the reckless pursuit of pleasure which meets man's love of beauty and happiness with the tawdry and the meretricious.

Within a man's own personality there is no lack of "thieves and robbers." There is his driving ambition which without the influence of Christ becomes, sooner or later, a destructive tyrant; there is his pride which insulates him from his neighbor and sows enmity between his group and another. Above all, there is his fear, rooted of course in pride and self-love, which drives out the milk of human kindness and which in its extreme forms makes him behave far worse than the animal creation. We have to face the fact that in the individual man as well as in society there have always been these disintegrating factors, the "thieves and robbers" who, though often unseen, are quietly at work. Yet wherever He is given the chance, there is the integrating factor, the Good Shepherd Himself, seeking to make men whole, seeking to integrate both human personality and the whole human family.

The problem of making men whole, of integrating them as persons and unifying them in a community, is much more difficult than some idealists might suppose. The "thieves and robbers," the disintegrating forces, have had very long innings. They are deeply entrenched, their cumulative infection is overwhelming, and they are by no means always recognized for what they are. It is quite literally a superhuman task to plunge into the welter of centuries of disintegration and begin to make men whole.

At the risk of repetition, it must be emphasized that what we are beginning to envisage nowadays is a much larger-scale and more widespread integration than our forefathers as a general rule imagined. The salvation of an individual soul is indeed important, but we are beginning to see that the work of the Good Shepherd goes deeper and wider than we ever supposed. It is true that His plan considers the importance of the single "sheep"; under the Good Shepherd the one sheep can be saved and "go in and go out and find pasture" (John 10:9). But the plan is far greater than that. There are the "other sheep" (John 10:16) at present astray, who must also be brought into the fold. It is not only the so-called contemporary pressures which make us feel that we are "all in this together"; to those who are sensitive to the breath of the Spirit it is surely God Himself who is widening our horizons, mentally and spiritually, and making us feel and see the breathtaking compass of His integrating purpose.

Nothing less than a worldwide principle of wholeness, a world-loving and world-loved King and Shepherd, will suffice for our modern need. In the past, so long as men were broken up into more or less self-contained units, it was not altogether impossible to secure an integration which was local and to some extent superficial. The rules and customs of a tribe, for example, the unquestioned but purely parochial authority of their king, priest, or leader produced such a limited "wholeness." In our own country, there sometimes existed in a village, for example, such a circumscribed integration. And no doubt in many countries a similar local harmony was often achieved. But the need today, as is obvious to anyone with eyes to see, is for something at once more penetrating and more far-reaching than that limited conception. Indeed, on examination we find that the apparent wholeness of little communities was due at least in part to fear of other communities; and the very loyalty which preserved the local cohesion would effectually prevent cooperation with similar communities. In our Lord's day, for example, there was a certain cohesive loyalty about the Jews which produced in both personality and community some magnificent results. Yet it was exclusive, "for Jews have no dealings with Samaritans" (John 4:9), and they regard the Gentiles with, at the best, a tolerant contempt. We hardly realize the explosive quality of St. Paul's inspiration when, under the influence of the new integrating force, he declared that in Christ there can be "neither Jew nor Greek, there can be neither bond nor free, there can be no male and female" (Galatians 3:28).

The Crucifixion

JESUS REGARDED HIS own approaching death as a bitter necessity. Yet we, like the disciples who "followed with fear in their hearts," as the Gospel tells us, may well feel puzzled as they. Why must the One whom they were beginning to recognize as God-in-human-form undergo such a frightful death? Surely, if ever this was a case for divine intervention, for the flashing down of the celestial army of rescue that men might know who had been in their midst. Yet nothing of the kind occurred. The travesty of justice took its course, and the Man who was God in human form was brutally flogged and nailed to a wooden cross to die in the blazing sun.

We can appreciate the heroism and we can feel something of the tragedy, but can we understand the necessity, the bitter necessity?

I think, in order to do this, we have to think a little of the nature of God and of man. So long as we are skirting round the edges of the Christian Faith, thinking of God as some vague distant Benevolence, we shall not see the clamant need for reconciliation between God and man. But once we attempt with our adult minds and hearts to lead a Christian life, we begin to see the difficulty. For the gulf between us and God is not merely an intellectual one—it is not that God is infinitely wise and we, by comparison, blundering fools, though that is true—but the real gulf lies in the moral realm. You and I, through our own sins and failures, as well as by the infection of the sins of other people, are separated from God by a moral gulf. All serious religions recognize this, and all of them attempt some bridgehead from sinful human nature towards the Beauty and Perfection of the Holiness of God. Yes, they all attempt bridgeheads, but just as it is impossible to build a bridge across a chasm without starting from both sides, so it proves impossible in this matter of a moral gulf to do more than erect a painful and desperate bridgehead, *unless Someone is also building from the other side*. And that is precisely what we believe Christ did for us men. Not only did He, who was by nature God, come down to be born as a human being, not only did He live a life of perfect sinlessness, not only did He give us the "blueprint" or "recipe" for happy and constructive living, but in Himself He built the Bridge to span the gulf between God and man. "God was in Christ reconciling the world unto Himself."

The whole of mankind is caught up in a vicious circle of sin, suffering, and death, and Jesus Christ, Himself God and Himself Man, deliberately allowed Himself to be caught up in that deadly process. Though personally He had never done anything but good, though personally He had had no dealings with any form of sin, He, as Representative Man (for that is what "Son of Man" means), took the rap for mankind. We cannot begin to understand what kind of horror and revulsion such an experience must have meant to Him. It was, of course, not merely the physical degradation and suffering, but the terrifying dark experience of allowing evil to close in upon Him and kill Him, that fills us with wonder and awe.

The Act of Reconciliation

IN ALL OUR MINDS, sometimes lurking deep beneath the conscious level, there lies a sense that there is this gulf between us and God, and that something ought to be done about it. We make our good resolutions, we turn over new leaves—or we try to laugh the whole thing off—but there remains the sense that we are a long way from God and that there is nothing that we can do to close the gap. Sometimes we feel a passing sympathy with those heathen religions which make sacrifices, or go through complicated rituals of atonement to make themselves right with God, but we of the twentieth century feel we have grown beyond that sort of thing, though we have not grown beyond the sense that something ought to be done to atone for our sins and failures.

When we look at the Cross, without sentimentality, but with a little thought and imagination, we realize that what we could never do, what we are always powerless to do, *has been done* by Christ. This is the Act of Reconciliation which we could never make, the Bridge which we could never build. No longer do we see God as the Fearful Judge isolated in splendid Majesty, but right down among us, taking upon Him our flesh and plunging into the heart of our insoluble difficulty. When we see what sort of a God the Cross reveals to us, it is no exaggeration to say that a revolution takes place in our thinking and our feeling. It is not too difficult to hurl defiance at a high and mighty God who, secure in His majesty, makes us mortals feel guilty and afraid. But it is impossible to be unmoved when we see our very Creator down in the sweat and dust of the arena, going to that awe-inspiring length to make the Reconciliation. It may come quietly into our hearts, or it may break over us like a wave, that the nature of God is not, as we supposed, that of a Tyrant, a Spoilsport, or a Jesting Fate, but Love— not sentimental love, but real Love, that would face the grim degradation of the Cross to reconcile us to Himself.

The Resurrection According to Paul

THE FIFTEENTH CHAPTER [of First Corinthians] which I have come to regard in some ways as the most important chapter in the New Testament . . . is the earliest evidence for the resurrection of Christ. We need to remind ourselves that so far there were no written gospels, and that these words were written some twenty years after the crucifixion of Jesus. There would still be many alive who knew and re- membered Him, and Paul lists some of those who saw Christ alive after his very public death. I was struck again by the "over five hundred Christians" who saw Jesus si- multaneously, "of whom," Paul comments, "the majority are still alive." The evidence for the Resurrection does not rest on hysterical visions in the half-light of early dawn but on actual "appearances," the last of which seems to have happened to Paul. I noticed the flat, matter-of-fact recital of known events. There is no attempt to persuade or prove, and certainly there is no artistic embellishment. Paul is, in effect, saying: these are the historic facts which we know.

Then, at verse 12, he does allow himself to be moved. Since the risen Christ convinced him, and since the risen Christ is the power behind the gospel he preaches, as well

as the author of the faith which has grown up in the unlikely soil of Corinth, how *can* anyone, even for the sake of
argument, deny that Christ really rose?

I confess that I was as much astonished as Paul that *Christians* should not believe in the life that is to follow this obviously incomplete and imperfect one. Since faith in the
resurrection of Christ and the sharing of his timeless life
has always been an integral part of the Gospel, I cannot
help wondering why quite a proportion of those who accept
Christianity stop short of its most valuable promise.

It may be that there is some lack of imagination. If we
speak loosely of "eternity," some people think that we
mean millions of years plus millions of years ad infinitum.
They do not seem able to grasp the fact that once we are
outside the time-and-space setup (in which we are in this
life inescapably confined), neither "time" nor "space" has
any meaning. There may be all kinds of "dimensions" of
which we are at present ignorant, and for which there are
no descriptive words.

But I believe Paul himself puts his finger on the nub of
the matter in verse 35 of this same chapter. Some people
then, as some people now, seemed to envisage this temporary corruptible body being magically revived, and to think
that this is what is meant by "resurrection." Of course it is
not. Paul is at pains to explain that even on this planet the
"body" which contains the life is adapted to the environment—fish, birds, animals are all different, while the "celestial bodies" to be observed in the sky are completely and
splendidly unlike anything earthly.

God gives us the "spiritual" body suitable for the new
environment for which we are destined as sons of God. We
can be sure of that, and the resurrection of Christ is our
guarantee. We can be equally sure that "the transitory could
never possess the everlasting" (verse 50). Indeed who
would wish for this old, weary, diseased, and possibly

maimed body to be somehow newly injected with life? We know perfectly well that human flesh eventually decays, quickly by fire or slowly by decomposition in the earth, whatever the "morticians" would have us believe.

Why, then, does Paul insist on a "body" at all? It is because he is concerned to defend the Christian belief in man's resurrection after the pattern of Christ's resurrection. The old Greek belief, and its Roman counterpart, held that once the body was dead the disembodied soul lived a miserable twilight existence in Hades. It was the place of shadows and shades, the dark and joyless limbo of the departed. The Hebrew idea of Sheol was very little different. Sadness, silence, and hopelessness seemed to brood over the life after death. The men and women of Corinth would probably have heard of both Hades and Sheol. They might also have heard vaguely of the Greek philosophers' concept of the immortality of the human soul.

But death was to men of those days the ultimate disaster. It may be that some of these Corinthians could not accept the miserable twilight of such places as Hades or Sheol and that the persistence of the "soul" seemed no more than a philosopher's speculation. It may be that to believe in annihilation at death seemed to them the best way to meet it.

This negative thinking Paul is determined to correct. The resurrection of Christ was always to him the key to the human dilemma. Christ had become man, Christ had died for man, and Christ had risen to open the door to the glories that human vocabulary has no words to describe. Paul knew that man's last enemy, death, was now defeated, and men would look forward, not to a shadowy half-life, but to a life fuller and more glorious than human imagination can conceive. No more nonsense, he urges, about what sort of "body" we shall possess when these mortal bodies perish. That we can safely leave to God, who has demonstrated the defeat of death by the raising up of Christ.

For me, the translator, this fifteenth chapter seemed alive and vibrant, not with pious hope, but with inspired certainty. Quite suddenly I realized that *no man had ever written such words before.* As I pressed on with the task of translation I came to feel utterly convinced of the truth of the Resurrection. Something of literally life-and-death importance had happened in mortal history, and I was reading the actual words of people who had seen Christ after his resurrection and had seen men and women deeply changed by his living power. Previously, although I had known something of the "comfort of the Scriptures" and had never thought them to be false, I must have been insulated from their reality simply because they were known as "Scripture." Now I was compelled to come to the closest possible terms with this writing, and I was enormously impressed, and still am. On the one hand, these letters were written over quite a period of years, but there is not the slightest discernible diminution of faith. And on the other hand, it was borne in upon me with irresistible force that these letters could never have been written at all if there had been no Jesus Christ, no Crucifixion, and no Resurrection.

The more I thought about it, the more unthinkable it became that any of this new, courageous, joyful life could have originated in any kind of concocted story or wishful thinking. There had been a stupendous Event, and from that was flowing all this strength and utter conviction.

The Resurrection According to Luke

STRANGELY ENOUGH, it was while translating that vibrant book commonly known as the Acts of the Apostles, and which I renamed the "Young Church in Action," that the full weight of Christian evidence, centered as it must be in the Resurrection, fell upon me with renewed force. But I must wait a little while before I expand this conviction. For the patient, careful Luke, with his sensitive "feeling" for words, has more to tell us about Christian beginnings. I had already come to the conclusion that he was a careful historian, the kind of man who would tactfully but firmly persuade people to tell him what they had actually seen and heard, and check his information. We do not know exactly when Luke became a Christian. Apparently, once he had embraced the Christian cause, he became Paul's close companion in all kinds of danger and hardship. But, if the records are to be trusted, and I believe they are, he was far more than "the beloved physician." He set himself out to write for Theophilus, a real or imaginary character, as true an account of the earthly life of Jesus as he could manage. When we come to his second work, the Acts, it is obvious that he has been asking further questions of eyewitnesses of events which he himself had not seen. Thus, in the opening chapter of Luke's second book, we get a more detailed and expanded version of what we commonly call the Ascension. Here I think the picture has been spoiled for us by some literal-minded people who confuse the noisy, wasteful, and expensive business of blasting a man into "space" with the quiet simplicity of the real acted parable of the Ascension. There is no connection between the two; you might just as profitably enquire about the actual candlepower used in the Transfiguration or of the light intensity, brighter than the noonday sun, which halted Saul in his tracks on his way to Damascus.

I know that it takes a little time for human minds to assimilate a stupendous new truth. Thus we find Jesus appearing and disappearing over a period of some six weeks. During this time he is not only teaching his disciples, but helping them to grow accustomed to the idea that he is *with* them, and indeed will be *in* them, whether he is visible or not. But eventually the time comes when he must show them as directly, simply, and kindly as possible that as a bodily presence, such as they knew in the streets and on the hills of Palestine, he is to be no more with them. What would more plainly and finally convey to the men of those days this departure than the simple event of the Ascension? There is no question of a "countdown" and a "blast-off"! In the act of blessing them, the man, whom they knew and loved, rose there on the hillside until "a cloud received him out of their sight." This is what they saw; this is what they later reported to Luke; but it is not to be explained or explained away in terms of modern physics. Nevertheless it must have been an extraordinarily satisfying experience for these early disciples, since they, according to Luke, "returned to Jerusalem with great joy." They knew now for certain that death had been conquered, they knew that their beloved Jesus was truly the Son of God, and ringing in their ears was the promise that they would be given power to go out and to tell the world.

I found Luke's account of the beginning of the young church strangely moving. This mere handful of early believers, who had deserted their Master the moment real danger threatened, and who had, apparently, taken so long to realize that he had really and demonstrably conquered death, are bidden to wait. They are convinced; they are full of joy. But they lack the power to breach the defenses of an unbelieving world. The story, all too familiar to many of us who have been Christians for years, is told with extraordinary simplicity and economy of words. There must be some God-given power given to that tiny band charged with the alarming (and seemingly impossible) task of "preaching the gospel to every creature." And there was, for the living Spirit of God came upon these men in a way no one could have anticipated. Luke is describing, perhaps thirty years later, something of what men told him had happened at that momentous Pentecost. I cannot believe that Luke, or anybody else, concocted such a story. It is superhuman but not magical, and I find it wholly credible. There is this curious mixture of the earthly and the heavenly, which is typical of most of the New Testament. We have not gone very far in reading the Acts when, in chapter 6, we come across a down-to-earth case of human grumbling, or possibly jealousy. Whereupon seven more men are chosen as "deacons," among them Stephen, the first to suffer death for his faith. But even here Luke has an eye for a small but significant detail. In verse 7 of the same chapter we read that "a great company of the priests were obedient to the faith." Frankly, I had never seriously considered this before. The established order of things ecclesiastical, which included "the priests," had always seemed to me to be implacably opposed to Jesus, and later to Paul, wherever he traveled to proclaim the gospel. Now I cannot believe that Luke made this up! It is one of those unexpected partial glimpses of truth which make the whole so convincing.

But as I continued to read Luke's fascinating story, I slowly realized that the message proclaimed was basically that of "Jesus and the Resurrection." (This was almost farcically true just before Paul preached, not altogether unsuccessfully, to the sermon-tasters on Mars Hill. Some Stoic and Epicurean philosophers thought he was proclaiming *two* "foreign deities," Jesus and Anastasis [resurrection!]). The young church had, apparently, no knowledge of what we nowadays call the Virgin Birth, or even of the Christmas story. The great point to them was that God had become a human being, had been publicly executed, and then had *conquered death.* He had shown himself to them alive "by many infallible proofs" (Acts I:3) and had even eaten and drunk with them! (Acts 10:41). Naturally they could never forget this, and, as the gospel was preached to the then-known world, "Jesus, the risen Lord" was the heart and core of the message. The resurrection of Jesus was, and indeed is, historic fact. I suppose I have studied the relevant documents, commentaries, and attempts to controvert the whole story as fully as most men, and I am utterly convinced that *this thing really happened*. I am deeply grateful to Luke for showing me that it was the resurrection from death of a man. God's chosen man, Jesus, which gave the early church its enormous drive, vitality, courage, and hope.

The Resurrection in the Gospels

THE STORIES OF the rising from the dead of the man Jesus are not mounted or arranged as evidence for any court of law—or for that matter for any critic. I should be highly suspicious of them if they were. People who are frightened and despairing, suddenly confronted with evidence which contradicts all their previous experience of life, can hardly be considered to be ideal witnesses. Wouldn't you be shaken to the marrow if a young man whom you had seen die publicly and in agony on Friday greeted you with a cheerful greeting on the following Sunday? Does it *matter* whether there was one "man in white" or two who spoke to the bewildered women at the opened sepulcher? Can we not understand that a woman, half-crazy with grief and with eyes nearly blind with weeping should mistake a male figure in the early morning light for the gardener? Have we never been so overwhelmed with grief or disappointment, or both, that we literally do not *see* anything else? I am therefore not in the least worried by the story of the walk to

Emmaus (recorded only by Luke, and possibly recovered by him in his patient researches). I see no difficulty in believing that the minds of Cleopas and his companion were so utterly preoccupied with the collapse of their hopes and dreams that they did not recognize Jesus. Obviously, all the time that they had been walking with him, their despair was melting and their faith in Jesus, God's Christ, was coming back to life. But the "psychological moment" came when they were relaxed at a friendly table, and a familiar gesture brought instant recognition. It all "clicked into place," as we say in modern slang, or, as Luke records, "their eyes were opened and they knew him." Now, no one makes up a story like this. No one ever has, or ever will. This rings true; this certainly happened.

There is an almost haphazard recording of the appearances of Jesus after his resurrection, which I find extraordinarily convincing. I think my favorite again occurs in Luke's work. When the two who were walking to Emmaus had rushed back to Jerusalem to report their astounding experience to the eleven, they found that they already knew that "the Lord is risen indeed and hath appeared to Simon." Again, according to Luke, while they are still talking excitedly, Jesus himself appears among them. They were, as we might say, scared out of their wits; they thought they were seeing a ghost. But Jesus reassures them, and as was his habit, he asks penetrating questions. "Why are you so worried? . . . Why do doubts arise in your minds? Look at my hands and my feet—it is really I myself! Feel me and see; ghosts have no flesh and bones, as you can see that I have." Then Luke makes his shrewd comment as a doctor and student of human nature. Some things are too good to be true, and the human mind cannot accept them at once. It is entirely natural to me that Luke should record that "they still could not believe it through sheer joy and were quite bewildered." Then follows this extraordinary, and in a way amusing, test of whether Jesus was really there in person. He asks them, "Have you anything here to eat?" We can imagine the frantic dash to a shelf or cupboard where they kept their food, and we can imagine that they saw no incongruity in offering him a piece of broiled fish and part of a honeycomb. But I myself cannot imagine that Jesus consumed this rather strange meal before their eyes without a smile! But this in a way clinched it; whoever heard of a ghost *eating?* Again, I find this is the kind of story which no man would invent, but which any man who was present would remember until his dying day. And Luke, bless him, records it.

John, writing considerably later, contents himself with remarking, "many other signs truly did Jesus in the presence of his disciples which are not written in this book" (John 20:30). We cannot help wishing he had written more.

Although it is clear that Jesus meant his friends to understand that he had truly conquered death and sometimes went to great pains to convince them of the fact (see especially John 20:27), even a cursory reading of the Gospel stories is enough to show that the "appearances" are not the same in quality. On some occasions Jesus, now the risen Christ, appears among his astonished disciples when they are met behind closed doors, and sometimes he appears in the open air. Apparently his visible presence could disappear instantly, yet apparently he could also make himself not only visible but tangible to human senses. In the earliest account of the Resurrection appearances, which Paul records in 1 Corinthians 15, Paul seems to make no distinction between different kinds of appearance. His own vision of the risen Lord is to him as valid as the experience of the Apostles, "the five hundred brethren assembled at once," and the others. Nevertheless I am pretty certain that, if pressed, Paul would be the first to admit that the appearances were different in kind. The important thing to him was that "this man Jesus" had been "raised" by God from the dead, and had been set above all power in heaven and earth.

It does not bother me in the least that the man whom God had proved to be his Christ, and to whom God had given "all power in heaven and earth" should use his "resurrection body" in any way that he chose. There are such things as visions, and there are hallucinations, but the more I study the evidence the more I am convinced that Jesus was raised from the dead, body and all, in a real sense, leaving an open tomb and empty grave clothes.

The Revolution of the Resurrection

EVEN THOUGH THE Gospels are not . . . biographies, they build up a picture of a man whose stature and quality are unsurpassed in history. Yet no man rescued him from humiliation, mockery, and a torturing death. No celestial rescue party intervened. This was not merely the end of all their hopes and dreams to the early Christians, but a cruel outrage to their sense of justice. If ever there was a case for divine intervention, surely it was here. Once, in a moment of inspiration, Simon Peter had said, "You are Christ, the Son of the Living God!" And we may fairly assume that the others had come to share this view to a greater or lesser extent. Yet it was not to a band of expectant hero worshipers that Jesus appeared, but to men and women stunned by bitter grief and shattering disappointment. We can only guess at the black cloud of disillusionment which must have swept over them. After this terrible, final, and public disaster they had, apparently, forgotten that he himself had foreseen and indeed forewarned them of what would happen.

It was against a background of broken hope and utter despair that the great miracle occurred. All four Evangelists spend quite a lot of their short narratives in recounting the betrayal, the mock trial, the final humiliations, and the criminal execution. I do not think this was done merely for dramatic effect. It was written to show that even the best of men could suffer in this evil world. It was written to show all who should follow Jesus that he was not God *pretending* to be a man, but God who had become a man.

Thus the resounding triumph of the Resurrection was all the more splendid and magnificent. Armed with no supernatural equipment, Jesus had conquered man's last enemy, death. He had shown beyond any possible doubt that the victory was complete. To live again was no longer a pious hope or a wishful thought; it was a certainty. No conspiracy, no trick, no hysterical vision was responsible for this new certainty. As Paul remarked crisply some years later to King Agrippa, "This thing was not done in a corner" (Acts 26:26).

The Ascension

IT HAS ALWAYS seemed to me that the Ascension of our Lord is something of a poor relation among the festivals of the Church year. I imagine that this is largely because the divine event is celebrated on a weekday, and unless one is a pupil at a school with Christian observances—when the holy day is chiefly remembered because it is a day's holiday—it is likely to pass almost unnoticed by many good Christian people, and its significance scarcely appreciated.

Paul was not merely uttering a truism when he said— "Now that he ascended, what is it but that he also descended first? . . ." If we really believe that human life was invaded from Heaven by God's becoming a human being, it is surely not unreasonable to believe that the complement to that celestial dive of rescue is an ascension back in triumph to Heaven. The man who was also God had accomplished his mission, he had founded the kingdom, he had affected the reconciliation between God and man, and he had defeated man's last enemy—death. The Ascension not only satisfies the mind by completing the divine work, but it also strengthens and encourages the Christian soul. . . .

Men of all religions, of even of none, speak of "high" ideals, "high" aspirations, or even of "high" positions of responsibility or command. This seems to be a normal human trait, even though it is logically absurd, quite as absurd as it is to call one musical note "higher" than another. It does not really matter that the man of prayer might lift up his eyes to the heavens in the northern hemisphere, while the man in the southern hemisphere lifts up his eyes in a completely opposite direction. The point really is that human beings look up to God and what Paul calls the "heavenly," whether they are aware that they live on a spherical globe or not. Thus it was natural for Jesus, his work accomplished, to leave his followers by this acted parable. The man whom the early Christians had seen die and rise again did not simply vanish from their sight, as he had done on several occasions since his resurrection, but visibly ascended. The simplest witness could understand the obvious meaning of this action, while the wisest could ponder long over its deeper significance.

There are two aspects of this, the last earthly action of Jesus Christ, on which I think we can profitably reflect. . . . The first is simply this: that Jesus, who was both man and God, was taking humanity in his own person into the heavenly realm. This, naturally, had never been done before. Of course it is true that the risen Christ was not in all respects the same person as the representative man who had died in agony on the cross. We have only to read the resurrection stories to realize this. Yet he had become a man, he had involved himself in the human predicament, and as the eldest of many sons he was taking humanity into the new, perfect world—which is not just another "layer" above the protective belts that lie around this planet, but a new dimension beyond time and space as we know them.

He left with the promise to those who believe in him that "where I am there ye may be also." And since flesh and blood cannot possibly survive in the eternal world, we are promised through the inspired words of Paul that "we shall all be changed" and we shall be given bodies of new quality which the new world will demand. (A fresh reading of the fifteenth chapter of the first epistle to the Corinthians will help our thinking here.)

This much I think I can fairly see and believe, and the Ascension of Christ after his triumphant resurrection is the historical guarantee for our faith.

But the second aspect of the Ascension puzzles me considerably. It is simply this: that Jesus Christ, even before his death, spoke of his return to the Father and said these enigmatic words—"I go to prepare a place for you." We cannot help wondering what this preparation could be. We have grown away from the idea, and rightly in my judgment, that Jesus Christ is, to put it crudely, the "cushion" between the angry Father and us sinful human beings. There can be no schizophrenia in the nature of God, and in any case the ascended Christ had made the reconciliation which we could never make. Behind those mysterious and dreadful words, "he hath made him to be sin for us who knew no sin" and "he should taste death for every man," there lies more than a hint of the personal cost of our redemption. But at the time of the Ascension this was over; the agony, the darkness, and the dereliction of Calvary had been endured; and the resurrection was the proof that the work was done. What now remains for the ascended Christ to do?

I think this promise of Christ's "preparation" for men was meant, and is meant, to convey comfort, love and reassurance. However sincerely we trust our Lord, however deeply we love him, there remains something alarming to the naked human soul who is transferred by death from this familiar sphere into the beauty and perfection of the eternal world. . . . We love and welcome flashes of beauty, truth and goodness, but who in his own imperfection could face their very presence? It is true, as Paul was inspired to write, that "eye hath not seen, nor ear heard . . . the things which God hath prepared for them that love him"; but anyone with any imagination at all can sense the shock to the imperfect when it meets the perfect, to the incomplete when it meets the complete. This is perhaps why we need these words of reassurance.

Without pressing the words too literally, surely we are meant to be both strengthened and reassured by Christ's promise. He who was God by nature became man by deliberate choice, and, having perfected his mission, he now takes the humanity which he shares with us into the world of unimaginable perfection. Whatever lies behind his mysterious promise of "preparation" surely he means that we shall be at home in the place which he has prepared. We may be amazed but we shall not be terrified; we may be dazzled but we shall not be blinded. And it is perfectly possible that the tears which God will wipe from our eyes will not only be tears of regret for our past failures but tears of joy and unspeakable relief.

I spoke above of Ascension Day having become a kind of poor relation. It should, in fact, remind us that in our Lord and Savior we have an infinitely rich relation! For he is rich in mercy, in love and in understanding. He has defeated all our enemies, and the welcome which he has prepared for those who love and trust him will certainly surpass our wildest dreams.

The Living Spirit of Truth in the New Testament

I BELIEVE IT TO be very important indeed that close examination of the New Testament should produce conviction of its truth. No one is going to take the trouble to read it if once the idea becomes accepted that all we have is a collection of myths—and that is what is suggested by some of our so-called experts. Thus the Christian Church (and by that I mean all the churches) is regarded by many as a collection of people blindly clinging to beliefs which everyone else knows are false and refusing to meet modern scientific truth. Obviously there are some Christians who are obscurantists in their outlook, but I have met a good many, of most denominations, in both England and America who are displaying the same Christian qualities as the people described in the New Testament. They are refusing to be secularized, and they are refusing to allow the state or humanism or anything else to occupy the place which belongs to God.

Naturally we cannot turn the clock back, and it would be stupid to pretend that life anywhere in today's world is the same as the life of New Testament times. But people are the same, and the basic problems of human relationships are the same. The Spirit which Jesus promised would lead his followers "into all truth" is very actively at work wherever he is allowed. Some of his work is painful in the extreme. There has often to be the breaking-up of old ways of thinking, the expansion of responsibility, and the checking of priorities. Anyone who opens his personality to the living Spirit takes a risk of being considerably shaken. It seems obvious to me that the Churches themselves are also being shaken, perhaps as they have not been for centuries.

But we need not fear. The Spirit of truth does not contradict himself. It is not that the essential faith revealed in the New Testament is shown to be wrong; it is much more that our eyes are opened and we see how much more deeply relevant that faith is to our modern days than we thought. So that we do not gain but lose if we dismiss what was written by the inspiration of the same Spirit as folktale or myth. He will certainly lead us into all truth, but he will not lead us into arrogance and a confusion between technical advance and spiritual wisdom. He will certainly help us to "communicate" the truth of God to other people, but he becomes our enemy the moment we attempt to modify the wisdom of God to fit the "cleverness" of the twentieth century. The stern words of Paul have a peculiar aptness to the modern situation when he says, "The foolishness of God is wiser than men" (1 Corinthians 1:25).

The Gospels

THE GOSPELS ARE NOT, in the modern sense, biographies. We have no idea of the physical stature or build of their chief subject, and no clue to his coloring. We do not know whether he had a powerful voice, although we may fairly infer that he was physically strong. Apart from one isolated incident, we have no information about his childhood, adolescence, or young manhood and no record of the influences which formed his character. If we are looking for biography in the modern sense, we are disappointed. Some, like the late Albert Schweitzer, came to the conclusion that we never could know Jesus as an historical figure. And quite a number of scholars today would hold much the same view. The most we can do is to understand the meaning behind the "myths" of the Hellenic-Semitic world of first-century Palestine. I cannot, as a translator, agree with this at all, except in one minor way, which I will return to later.

Suppose you are, as I was, translating with the mind emptied as far as possible of preconception. You cannot help noticing the differences between the hurried, almost breathless style of Mark, where almost everything seems to happen "straight away," and the much more elaborate Gospel of Matthew, who has a very definite purpose in view—to convince the Jews that Jesus was indeed the Messiah of whom the Old Testament prophets had spoken. Quite different again is the work of Luke, who appears to have made diligent research and unearthed some stories of Jesus which none of the other Evangelists mentions. Here, uniquely, are set down the concern of Jesus for women, for foreigners, and for the underprivileged. To me it had all the marks of careful writing. And then came the problematical fourth Gospel, which is a work of quite different character.

Suppose that you have spent many hundred hours in putting these four widely differing accounts of some of the sayings and doings of the man Jesus into today's English. Do you find yourself so confused that you conclude that there was no such person at all? I take leave to doubt it. It is, in my experience, the people who have never troubled seriously to study the four Gospels who are loudest in their protests that there was no such person. I felt, and feel, without any shadow of doubt that close contact with the text of the Gospels builds up in the heart and mind a character of awe-inspiring stature and quality. I have read, in Greek and Latin, scores of myths, but I did not find the slightest flavor of myth here. There is no hysteria, no careful working for effect, and no attempt at collusion. These are not embroidered tales: the material is cut to the bone. One sensed again and again that understatement which we have been taught to think is more "British" than Oriental. There is an almost childlike candor and simplicity, and the total effect is tremendous. No man could ever have invented such a character as Jesus. No man could have set down such artless and vulnerable accounts as these unless some real Event lay behind them.

Thus the only small point which I will concede to the demythologizers is that several times I got the impression that the first three Evangelists, naturally enough, did not quite realize what a world-shaking happening they were describing. But how could they? Their view of the world was small; their knowledge of history was limited. They did not know even what Paul knew of contemporary life around them. It is easy for us to feel that these men were ignorant peasants compared with ourselves, who have advanced in knowledge over nearly two thousand years. If we do, we underestimate their intelligence and overestimate our own. Obviously they could not have anything approaching our historical perspective, but against this we must set the fact that they were living very much nearer to the actual point of time when Jesus was alive. There seems singularly little point in their concocting mythical stories about someone who never lived when violent persecution against those who followed the way of Jesus was well under way.

When I say that the first three Gospels at any rate are not biographies in the modern sense at all, I do not mean to say for one moment that I regard them as untrue. On the contrary, I believe them to be the verbal distillation of some of the things which Jesus said and did which the early Evangelists felt constrained to put down in writing. It is impossible at this stage to say what their original sources were, and do not let us forget that in no case have we an original manuscript or anything like it. But from the major manuscripts and from the thousands of minor ones, the textual experts are able to reconstruct with fair certainty what the Evangelists wrote in the first instance. One thing is perfectly clear: these men were not in a conspiracy together, or they would have been careful to avoid minor contradictions and discrepancies. The scholars who work out with enormous pains, through the evidence of style and vocabulary as well as from the content, the sources from which the Evangelists worked are called form critics. Of course, the whole business of form criticism is as absorbing and exciting as the best of detective stories, and I think it would surprise the average layman to know, for example, to what lengths the form critics will go in order to "prove" that some part of Luke's Gospel belonged to another period of time, or indeed to another author than the rest of it.

I should not like it to be thought that I want to belittle the work of the form critics, even though I sometimes cannot resist a smile at the way their views have changed over the last thirty years. But to me, as a translator, their work was largely irrelevant. I was dealing with material which was startlingly alive, and I could not really be overmuch bothered whether Matthew "borrowed" part of his Gospel story from Mark, or whether he and Mark shared a common source of written or spoken information which the critics call "Q." I know it is a shock to us today, and perhaps especially if we are professional writers and conscious of the laws of copyright, but it was not in the least strange in the first century A.D. to say that a gospel was "according to Matthew," even though it might contain sentences which were not written by Matthew at all. As long as the incident or the teaching was in keeping with the main stream which he had established, it seemed perfectly all right to the early Church to include it under Matthew's name. . . .

What seems to have happened, and in this I think all Christian scholars agree, is that the first three Evangelists wrote down what had previously been an oral tradition. This is no more than intelligent guesswork, but it seems likely that in the early days of the Christian community there was no need to write down the stories of what Jesus said and did, especially as many Christians were apparently expecting his early personal return. But what is not a guess but a fact is the fantastic retentiveness of the Oriental mind. Stories are told by word of mouth again and again, and no verbal deviation or embellishment is allowed. It is a phenomenon rather like that which children exhibit when they are very young and have their favorite bedtime story. It must not vary in the slightest detail from the familiar pattern. Strangely enough, only this very year I have been in contact with a friend who worked for some twenty-five years in business in Malaya. He found to his astonishment that conversations of twenty years ago and more could be recalled perfectly, mistakes, faulty pronunciations, and all, even though he himself had forgotten everything but the merest outline of such talk. Now this, I am told, would have been true of the Mediterranean world, and to me it seems most likely that it is the recollection of these gems of speech and action which the first three Evangelists record. This would account for the loose chronology, for we are reading not history in the modern sense but events and sayings treasured and remembered over a generation.

If we accept that the Evangelists, or at any rate the first three, wrote down various oral traditions which had been passed on with scrupulous accuracy over the years, we shall be spared many unnecessary headaches. Is it not reasonable to suppose that Jesus gave his teaching in slightly different forms on various occasions to different groups of people and that these were separately remembered and cherished? Before the days of mass communication (and that was not long ago) the prophet, preacher, or politician was bound to repeat his message again and again. What he said would be couched in compressed, intelligible, and memorable terms, but no one need suppose that he always used precisely the same words with parrot-like precision.

It is probable that Jesus spoke in Aramaic (a popular form of Hebrew), and if this is so, then the Evangelists had the extremely difficult job of listening to slightly varying accounts of the same, or similar, incidents and then setting them down in the widely understood Greek of the time. They were not reporters in the modern sense, nor were they preparing a statement for any court of law. They were simply setting down in writing what had till then been memorized and repeated by word of mouth. It is highly unlikely that we shall get any more information about the life and teaching of Jesus than we have already. In a sense this is tantalizing; what would we not give for a full-scale biography of this extraordinary man? How immensely valuable would be accurate descriptions of all that he ever said, as well as a detailed account of the events of his life. Why, we may plaintively ask, are we left almost completely in the dark about the childhood and young manhood of Jesus? Why have we no information (which would be regarded as essential in any modern biography) about the formative influences which produced such a matchless character? Why do we know almost nothing of the period between what we commonly call the Resurrection and the Ascension? What was it that the now risen Christ then taught to his followers about the "things pertaining to the Kingdom," as Luke describes them with such maddening brevity in the first chapter of the Acts? The plain answer is that we do not know.

The discovery of many papyri written in the same kind of

Greek as the New Testament has certainly illuminated our understanding of many words and expressions of that time. The Dead Sea Scrolls may well fill in more of our knowledge of Palestinian life of about the time of Jesus. But it is highly unlikely that the small esoteric group who copied and preserved the scrolls will shed any fresh light upon the actual historic life of Jesus or even, as some suggest, of John the Baptist. . . .

The fourth Gospel . . . is different in style, in vocabulary, and in "atmosphere." Instead of the true nature of Jesus being discovered in the course of his ministry, it is asserted at the beginning. Almost the whole of the story is set in Jerusalem. There is little mention of the extensive healing ministry of mind and body which the first three Evangelists record. Instead of short parables, we have quite lengthy discourses. There are times (inevitably, since New Testament Greek did not use quotation marks) when we are not sure whether we are reading the remembered words of Jesus himself or the comment of the Evangelist. Nevertheless the impact of the whole Gospel is, one is tempted to say, greater than the other three put together. The author plainly knew Jesus and had had time to think and meditate on the significance of the "Word becoming flesh." Whether he knew the existing Gospels we do not know, but I do not get the impression that John was writing a deliberate correction. The feeling is that a man of more maturity and deeper insight is giving his account. He is in effect saying, "This is how I saw and heard Jesus Christ, and this is the significance of his coming to this earth." The result is the portrait of a character in no way different from the sketches supplied by Matthew, Mark, and Luke, but carrying an even deeper authority.

Naturally I have read a good number of commentaries on John's Gospel, and I am fairly familiar with the difficulties of deciding who was the author. I also know of the hard task awaiting anyone who tries to fit this work into a "harmony" with the other Gospels. But I was not primarily concerned with this sort of thing. My work was to translate for, not to confuse, the modern reader.

The Letters

I WAS, AND INDEED AM, impressed by the fact that the New Testament letters were written not in some holy retreat but sometimes from prison, sometimes from ordinary, probably Christian homes. Moreover, they were written to people who were called to live Christian lives in a thoroughly pagan world. Moral standards of all kinds were low, and there was nothing remotely resembling a Christian public opinion. There were no Sundays, no church buildings, and very little leisure for most people. Slavery was, of course, everywhere, and so was dire poverty and unrelieved sickness and disease. The great persecutions had not yet started, but the smaller ones had. A man could lose not only his friends but his livelihood in a place like Ephesus if it became known publicly that he did not believe in the goddess Diana. A man could easily be looked at askance if he disowned the local gods, and he could be considered very odd if he broke with his previous companions in alcoholic revelings. And it could have been very easy to frame a charge against a man who set Jesus Christ above the Emperor of the Roman Empire.

It was against such a background of mixed paganism that the Christian faith began to grow and expand. Even if I were not myself a convinced Christian, I should find it impossible to explain this strange phenomenon. If we had records of a few emotional meetings, the effects of which were merely transient, we could write the whole Christian movement off as one of those passing waves of superstition which did from time to time disturb the pagan world. But we have no such thing: we have as good, solid evidence of a strong and growing faith as any historian could require. Let us, for a moment, discount the Gospel stories as written-up histories of a hero long since dead. (I do not myself think of the four Gospels like this, as I hope to show.) Even without the evidence of the books attributed to the four Evangelists, we have the strongest possible evidence for the early days of Christianity from the letters of Paul, James, Peter, and John. It is *letters* which are of unique value to the historian who is trying to record the actual events of any period. Newspapers, and before them broadsheets and pamphlets, naturally have their worth, but they are likely to be slanted one way or another. But if the historian can lay his hands upon a packet of letters, he has priceless evidence for the period of which he is writing. For letters, speaking generally, are not written with any political axe to grind, nor are they usually written for posterity. They reflect accurately the times in which they are written.

So it is with the New Testament Epistles. I doubt very much whether any of their writers had any idea that he was writing "Holy Scripture." For the most part it was *"ad hoc"* writing: a particular situation, or even the behavior of a particular person or group, called for the writing of the letter. Yet all of them, from their different points of view, bear witness to the growing of a new society of men and women quite different from the Greek, Roman, Jewish, or pagan pattern. The whole movement is based on the fact (about which no New Testament writer argues) that Jesus Christ was God and man. He is now "the Lord," and every system of thinking and every way of action must be decided not merely by reference to his example and teaching but by the leading of his active living Spirit.

As I continued this close association with the New Testament Epistles (on one full morning each week, for there was plenty of other work to be done!), I found an extraordinary unanimity of spirit. I say "extraordinary" because superficially Paul, James, John, and Peter are poles apart in temperament, and widely different in their presentation of the Christian gospel. But this difference is only superficial; it soon becomes plain that they are all speaking of the same thing, and, further, that their messages are complementary rather than contradictory. I have heard professing Christians of our own day speak as though the historicity of the Gospels does not matter—all that matters is the contemporary Spirit of Christ. I contend that the historicity does matter, and I do not see why we, who live nearly two thousand years later, should call into question an Event for which there were many eyewitnesses still living at the time when most of the New Testament was written. It was no "cunningly devised fable" but an historic irruption of God into human history which gave birth to a young church so sturdy that the pagan world could not stifle or destroy it.

The Greatness of Paul

WHEN I STARTED translating some of Paul's shorter letters I was at first alternately stimulated and annoyed by the outrageous certainty of his faith. It was not until I realized afresh what the man had actually achieved and suffered, that I began to see that here was someone who was writing, not indeed at God's dictation, but by the inspiration of God himself. Sometimes you can see the conflict between the Pharisaic spirit of the former Saul (who could say such grudging things about marriage and insist upon the perennial submission of women) and the Spirit of God, who inspired Paul to write that in Christ there is neither "Jew nor Greek . . . male nor female"!

Paul had, and still has, his detractors. There are those who say he is like the man who says, "I don't want to boast, but . . ."—and then proceeds to do that very thing! Very well then, but let us look at his list of "boasting." We have only to turn up 2 Corinthians 2:23–27. Has any of us gone through a tenth of that catalogue of suffering and humiliation? Yet this is the man who can not only say that in all these things we are more than conquerors, but can also "reckon that the sufferings of this present time are not worthy to be compared with the glory which shall be revealed in us" (Romans 8:18). Here is no armchair philosopher, no ivory-tower scholar, but a man of almost incredible drive and courage, living out in actual human dangers and agonies the implications of his unswerving faith. . . . I myself found as I studied [Paul's] writings that his mind was far more accurate than I had thought, and his imagination quite extraordinary in a man of such immense moral and physical courage. I would further say that we moderns tend to underestimate the intelligence of people like Paul. Because such a man had never seen a bicycle, a typewriter, or a television set, we, perhaps unconsciously, look down on him as living in some sort of twilight ignorance. We forget that he lived in point of time very close to the historic events described in the New Testament, and that he had plenty of opportunity to check their authenticity from many eyewitnesses. We forget, too, that he knew the philosophies of Greece not merely as textbook subjects but as systems of thought being taught and practiced in his day. When he wrote to the Colossians and warned them of "philosophy and vain deceit," he was not being anti-intellectual. He knew from observation as well as from personal knowledge of human beings that philosophy, however attractive intellectually, is sterile and impotent when it comes to changing human disposition.

Conversion of the Corinthians

THE LETTER WHICH really struck me a blow from which I have never recovered was the one popularly known as First Corinthians. Let me explain. I had been doing some background reading, and I was reminded that Corinth was a byword, even in those wicked old days, for every kind of vice and depravity. The Greeks, as usual, had a word for it, and "to Corinthize yourself" was to live with the candle alight at both ends, with all scruples and principles thrown aside, and every desire indulged to the full. Because of its geographical position—Corinth was easily reached by sea, and was a most important port in the East-West Mediterranean traffic—it had a very mixed population with a large number of travelers, traders, and hangers-on. It was probably not intrinsically any more wicked than any other seaport, but its reputation for sexual license had largely grown because it had been for hundreds of years a center for the organized worship of the Goddess of Love (first Aphrodite and now, in Roman times, Venus). As always happens where there is such a widespread sexual license, there sprang up a host of vicious fellow travelers—greed, blackmail, cheating, slander, perversion, and the rest.

I had a fair picture of the sort of place it must have been, and indeed of what an unlikely place it must have seemed for the founding of a Christian church, when I suddenly came across the eleventh verse of the sixth chapter. Paul has just recounted some of the more repulsive sins to which human beings can sink, and has assured his hearers that the Kingdom of God cannot be the possession of people like that, when suddenly he writes, AND SUCH WERE SOME OF YOU!

I had never realized what an astonishing piece of Christian evidence this is. No one doubts that this is an authentic letter of Paul, probably written some ten years before the first Gospel was set down. And here, to people living in this center of idolatry and all kinds of human depravity, Paul can write, "and such were some of you"! What, I ask, and shall continue to ask of my non-Christian friends, is supposed to have changed these men and women so fundamentally? The personality of Paul? The most casual reading of his two surviving letters to Corinth will quickly show that even among his converts he was not universally admired. It seems obvious that something very unusual had happened and was happening. People, sometimes the most unlikely people, were being converted in heart and mind by *something*. To Paul and his fellow Apostles it was plainly the invasion of the human spirit by God's own Spirit. The power required to convert and to sustain the new life *naturally* was to Paul another manifestation of the power which God showed in raising Jesus from the dead. The "fruits of the Spirit" which Paul lists in the fifth chapter of his letter to the Galatians are not the result of fearful effort and tormenting self-denial. They are fruits: they grow naturally, once the living Spirit of God is allowed to enter a man's inner being.

Nine New Testament Serendipities

Just over two hundred years ago, in 1754 to be precise, Horace Walpole coined the word "serendipity," which has now come to be accepted into our language. The word, which is derived from the ancient name for Ceylon, is defined as "the faculty of making happy and unexpected discoveries by accident." Before I go on to discuss the work of translating the Gospels I feel I must mention some of the "happy and unexpected discoveries" which I made in the translation of the Epistles.

"Rich in Mercy"

THE FIRST ONE I will mention, which of course may all the time have been no secret to anybody else, was the expression "rich in mercy" (Ephesians 2:4). This struck me as a positive jewel. Just as we might say that a Texas tycoon is "rich in oil," so Paul writes it as a matter of fact that God is "rich in mercy." The pagan world was full of fear, and the Christian gospel set out to replace that fear of the gods or the fates, or even life itself, with love for and trust in God. "Rich in mercy" was good news to the ancient world and it is good news today.

"Casting All Your Care"

I THINK THE IDEA of God's personal care for the individual came upon me with a similar unexpected strength when I came to translate 1 Peter 5:7, which reads in the Authorized Version, "Casting all your care upon him; for he careth for you." In one sense it is quite plain that God wants us to bear responsibility; it is a false religion which teaches that God wants us to be permanently immature. But there is a sense in which the conscientious and the imaginative can be overburdened. This familiar text reminded me that such overanxiety can be "off-loaded" onto God, for each one of us is his personal concern. The "text" is commonplace enough, perhaps too commonplace, for it was not until I had to translate it that I realized something of its full force. The word used for "casting" is an almost violent word, conveying the way in which a man at the end of his tether might throw aside an intolerable burden. And the Christian is recommended to throw this humanly insupportable weight upon the only One who can bear it and at the same time to realize that God cares for him intimately as a person. "He careth for you" is hardly strong enough and I don't know that I did much better in rendering the words, "You are his personal concern." The Greek words certainly mean this, but probably more. It is not the least glory of the Christian gospel that the God revealed by Jesus Christ possesses wisdom and power beyond all human imagining but never loses sight of any individual human being. It may seem strange to us, and it may seem an idea quite beyond our little minds to comprehend, but each one of us *matters* to God. It is of course the same sense of intimate concern which Jesus expressed poetically when he assured us that even the hairs on our head are numbered. It is the kind of inspired truth of which we have continually to remind ourselves, if only because life so often apparently contradicts it.

"Fear and Trembling"

I HAD FOR SOME time been worried about the expression "fear and trembling." It did not seem likely to me that Paul in writing to the Philippians could have meant literally that they were to work out their salvation in a condition of anxiety and nervousness. We all know that fear destroys love and spoils relationships, and a great deal of the New Testament is taken up with getting rid of the old ideas of fear and substituting the new ideas of love and trust. I realized that the Greek word translated "fear" can equally well mean "reverence" or "awe" or even "respect," but I was bothered about the "trembling." Surely the same Spirit who inspired Paul to write to Timothy that "God hath not given us the spirit of fear; but of power and of love and of a sound mind" could not also have meant us to live our entire lives in a state of nervous terror. I came to the conclusion, a little reluctantly, that the expression "in fear and trembling" had become a bit of a cliché, even as it has in some circles today. As I went on translating I found that this must be the case. For when Paul wrote to the Corinthians and reported that Titus had been encouraged and refreshed by their reception of him, he then went on to say that the Corinthian Christians received him with "fear and trembling" (2 Corinthians 7:15). Now this makes no sense, unless it is a purely conventional verbal form implying proper respect. For, little as we know of Titus, we cannot imagine any real Christian minister being encouraged and refreshed by a display of nervous anxiety. We get the same phrase occurring again in Paul's advice to Christian slaves (Ephesians 6:5), where the context makes it quite clear that faithfulness and responsibility are much more what Paul means than "fear and trembling." This much became plain, and then I realized that when Paul really did mean the words to be taken literally he amplified them to make sure they would be properly understood. I think we sometimes imagine that the incredibly heroic Paul suffered from no human weaknesses, except for the "thorn in the flesh" about which all New Testament commentators have written (2 Corinthians 12:7). But if we turn to 1 Corinthians 2:3, we find Paul writing that, "I was with you in weakness, and in fear, and in much trembling." Now this is a different thing altogether. Here we have a man honest enough to admit that he was frightened and that he was, or had been, ill. "Fear and trembling" here are perfectly legitimate. It is only when they are used as a phrase almost without literal meaning that we begin to feel uncomfortable.

"Pressed Out of Measure"

THIS LEADS ME to another heartening discovery, which I made in 2 Corinthians, chapter 1, verses 8 and following. I had not previously realized that even a man of such indomitable courage as Paul, filled as he undoubtedly was with the Spirit of the living God, could nevertheless be "pressed out of measure, above strength, insomuch that we despaired even of life." We lesser mortals, who live infinitely less adventurous lives, may sometimes experience something of this pressure. It is not that we, any more than Paul, despair of God as far as the ultimate outcome is concerned. But we can be overcome by the most terrifying darkness and reduced to a sense of inadequacy amounting to near desperation. Again, it was not until I came to the close study of this passage that I realized under what fearful pressure Paul must at times have been. I further came to see that the "stiff upper lip" business is not necessarily Christian; it sounds much more like a throwback to the Stoics than to early Christianity. For although the New Testament abounds in advice to men to be strong and to master their fears, it does not consider it disgraceful, for example, that a man might be moved even to tears, not indeed for himself but because he cared deeply for others. The letters tell no story of idealized human beings but reflect the life of people who are changed but by no means yet perfect.

"Quit You Like Men"

AT SOME STAGE in my life as a Christian I must have heard the total depravity of man heavily emphasized. I do not think I ever personally accepted this, because ordinary observation showed a good deal of kindness and generosity produced by people whether they had religious faith or not. But I have found among gatherings of Christians of various denominations a minority who seemed to get a perverse delight in this emphasis on man's utter hopelessness. And indeed we have not got to look far into devotional literature, whether Protestant or Catholic, to come across the idea that man is hopelessly sinful and incapable of good without the operation of the grace of God. . . . Now, to my joy, I found two delightful instances which could be quoted against the detractors of humanity if, as they sometimes do, they want to indulge in a text-slinging match! One comes from the first Epistle of John, where the writer reminds his hearers that no one should deceive them by any clever talk: "The man who lives a consistently good life is a good man as surely as God is good." This truth is no more and no less than the saying of Christ himself when He said, "You will recognize them by their fruit; a good tree cannot produce bad fruit, any more than a bad tree can produce good fruit." This was a pleasant refreshment, but there was another, wholly unexpected one at the end of the first Epistle to the Corinthians (16:13), where Paul urges his converts in the words "Quit you like men." (May I say in passing that these words from the Authorized Version are totally meaningless to the vast majority of young people.) The literal translation is, of course, "Be *men*." Now if it is true that man is so steeped in iniquity and incapable of goodness as some, especially in past centuries, would have us believe, there is no sense whatever in Paul's advice. But if it is true that the image of God is still present in man, however much it has been distorted or disfigured by evil, then it makes the most encouraging sense to be told to live like a man. At any rate, I must put it on record that this is the effect the inspired words had upon me.

"Everyone That Loveth ...
Knoweth God"

A SIMILAR PLEASANT "DISCOVERY" came in 1 John 4:7, in the words "everyone that loveth is born of God, and knoweth God." Again, this inspired truth had naturally been there all the time, but I don't think I had ever heard a sermon preached on it. Throughout my years of experience it had struck me that the things that were really admirable in human behavior were those inspired by love. I had also noticed, like many others, that people could exhibit most remarkable compassionate love without any great religious profession, or indeed with none at all. But if it is true, as John declares, that "God is love," it would make sense that any action that sprang from love had its origin in God. It would also mean that those who did give themselves in love to others did in fact "know God," however loudly they might protest their agnosticism. I have never been happy with any ecclesiastical or theological system in which correctness of belief was of paramount importance. It is only too easy for some men to build up a certain theological structure which includes them and excludes others. But what we really believe in our heart of hearts may be quite different from what we outwardly profess. I saw then, and I have seen nothing in life to disturb this view, that when a man acts in response to love and compassion he is responding to God *whatever he thinks or says.* Conversely the man who refuses to become involved in the troubles and burdens of his fellows is rejecting God, however religious his outward profession may be.

"Now Are We the Sons of God"

"BELOVED," WROTE JOHN, "now are we the sons of God, and it doth not yet appear what we shall be: but we know that, when he shall appear, we shall be like him; for we shall see him as he is" (1 John 3:2). These words, familiar as I think they must have been to me for years, were yet another shock for me as I came to translate them. For what would normally be sheer effrontery, or even blasphemy, is here written with cool confidence and authority. No one to my knowledge has ever written like these New Testament writers. Yet I was constantly aware that I was dealing not with exhortations or homilies but with letters written to people living in the midst of this world's business, people who were tempted and tried as we are, blinkered and frustrated and limited just as we are, yet with the same unquenchable flame of hope in their hearts as Christians have today. The material in this single verse is quite extraordinarily compressed; there is enough here for half a dozen useful sermons! But it is the *authority* which stabs the spirit broad awake. Paul and John wrote because they *knew*. The Christian revelation was not to them a tentative hypothesis, but the truth about God and men, experienced, demonstrated, always alive, and powerful in the lives of men. The whole Christian pattern had to be lived against pagan darkness and frequently overt hostility. It required superhuman qualities to survive. Of course there were casualties—Demas was not the first nor the last deserter—but the amazing thing to me is that the Christian Gospel took root and flourished in many different, and indeed unlikely, places.

"Count It All Joy"

THERE WAS ANOTHER unexpected treasure waiting for me in the letter of James. I suppose we all look upon the disappointments and pains of this life as somehow hostile to us. We either fight, or we grimly endure. It was therefore a salutary surprise to me to discover that James recommends his Christian brothers to *welcome* the assorted trials and troubles to which we are all exposed. "Count it all joy," he writes, "when you fall into divers [all kinds of] temptations" (1:2). Frankly I had never even thought of thus turning our apparent losses into real gains! But I am convinced that it is the right attitude to adopt. This is no question of "being a martyr," as we said when we were children, but of accepting suffering and loss as an integral part of life. I think we moderns are influenced more than we know by current modes of thinking which assume that we have a "right" to be happy, a "right" to live without pain, and somehow, a "right" to be shielded from the ills which flesh is heir to. Evidently the early Christians thought no such thing. They quite plainly took it as an honor to suffer for Christ's sake, and here the advice is to accept all kinds of troubles, whether they are apparently for Christ's sake or not, as friends instead of resenting them as intruders. Now I know that this kind of teaching can easily degenerate into an unhealthy and perverse wallowing in trouble. But this is not, I think, the early Christian intention. It is just as much a Christian duty to rejoice with those who rejoice as it is to weep with those who weep; it is as important to enjoy what God has richly given to us as it is to accept good humoredly and patiently the troubles, setbacks, disappointments, and griefs which are also part of the human pattern.

"If Our Heart Condemn Us"

I HAVE KEPT THE best until last. It occurs in John's first letter, chapter 3, verse 20. Like many others, I find myself something of a perfectionist, and if we don't watch ourselves this obsession for the perfect can make us arrogantly critical of other people and, in certain moods, desperately critical of ourselves. In this state of mind it is not really that I cannot subscribe to the doctrine of the Forgiveness of Sins, but that the tyrannical super-Me condemns and has no mercy on myself. Now John, in his wisdom, points out in inspired words, "If our heart condemn us, God is greater than our heart, and knoweth all things." This is a gentle but salutary rebuke to our assumption that we know better than God! God, on any showing, is infinitely greater in wisdom and love than we are and, unlike us, knows all the factors involved in human behavior. We are guilty of certain things, and these we must confess with all honesty, and make reparation where possible. But there may be many factors in our lives for which we are not really to blame at all. We did not choose our heredity; we did not choose the bad, indifferent, or excellent way in which we were brought up. This is naturally not to say that every wrong thing we do, or every fear or rage to which we are subject today, is due entirely to heredity, environment, and upbringing. But it certainly does mean that we are in no position to judge ourselves; we simply must leave that to God, who is our Father and "is greater than our heart, and knoweth all things." It is almost as if John is saying, "If God loves us, who are we to be so high and mighty as to refuse to love ourselves?"

Similes and Metaphors in the New Testament

THERE IS AN idea current among some New Testament scholars that people like Paul had a primitive system of thought—that theirs was a three-decker universe, with "heaven" above, "hell" below, and "earth" in between. For myself I seriously doubt this. In the intensive reading which translation requires I formed the strong impression that, far from trying to fit ideas of God into any preconceived concept, Paul is struggling with human words to express something of the wonders which, he senses, lie beyond observable life. To him it is the things which are seen that are temporal; it is the unseen things which are eternal. I find it hard to be patient with modern critics who assume that when Paul speaks of Christ's ascending "up on high" or when he urges the Colossians to "seek those things which are above, where Christ sitteth at the right hand of God," he is really talking of some location a certain number of miles above the earth's surface. There is a disquieting confusion of thought here. I think I can understand the Russian astronaut who is reputed to have said on his return from orbit that now he knew that there was no God, since he had been out in space and there was no one there. This shows merely a peasant's-eye view of religion. But there are several modern writers who pour scorn upon any idea of God being *up* or *above*. They are confusing literal spatial position with a mental image which must be common to nearly all thinking human beings. Why should we talk of *high* ideals or a *high* purpose? Why should we talk of a *rise* in salary? Why should sales be *soaring*? Why should a boy be promoted from the *lower* to the *upper* fifth form? Why does an important person in our judiciary sit in a *high* court? And so we could go on. It is a common and quite understandable symbolic way of speaking, and naturally the converse of it is equally true. For example, in ordinary speech a man may *fall* in our estimation, a failing business is fast going *downhill,* some people are of *low* intelligence, and some unfortunates have sunk to the *depths,* etc.

As I studied Paul's letters I became convinced that he uses expressions of height and depth as useful symbols but not as geographical locations. When, for example, he writes that, "God raised Christ from the dead and set him at his own right hand in the heavenly places, far above all principality and power, and might, and dominion, and every name that is named, not only in this world, but also in that which is to come," does anyone seriously imagine that Paul, or the Ephesian Christians to whom he was writing, thought of this exaltation as being measurable in physical terms? Again, in the same letter to Ephesus, when Paul asserts that the Christian's real battle is against spiritual rather than physical enemies and mentions "spiritual wickedness in high places," does anyone seriously suggest that Paul meant demonic goings-on at the Emperor's court? Of course not! To Paul there was the heavenly reality which at present we may sense but not see, and the earthly reality which is discernible by the senses but doomed, like all creation, to ultimate decay. The "bright blue sky" stuff belongs to Victorian piety and not to the New Testament.

I feel I must record here my sense of injustice that the Christian religion should be singled out as a target for criticism because it uses, and is bound to use, "picture language." We all do it every day of our lives, and we are none the worse for it. No one blames the accountant for talking of a "balance," the economist for speaking of "frozen assets," the electronics engineer for talking of a magnetic "field," the traffic controller for referring to a "peak" period, the electrical engineer for speaking of "load-shedding," or the town-planner for talking of a "bottleneck." Not one of these words is literally true, but each conveys quickly, and pretty accurately, an idea which can be readily understood. I cannot see why we, who accept hundreds of such usages in everyday speaking and writing, should decide that an expression such as "seated at the right hand of the Father" is either literally true or totally false.

But just as there is a real situation behind each of the shorthand "pictures" which I have given above, so there is a reality behind every Christian expression. Because picture language is sometimes used, it does not follow that the actual events are unhistorical or "mythical." The strange thing to me is that so few New Testament expressions need explanation. There are obvious exceptions: the Epistle to the Hebrews was especially written for the Hebrew mind and necessarily contains many ideas and expressions which are strange to the non-Jew. But on the whole the technical expressions are few and the "pictures" easily understood. Given a good translation, there is little in the New Testament letters which the modern reader will find dated or irrelevant. Indeed, as I said in a slightly different context above, I have literally hundreds of letters written from all parts of the English-speaking world which prove this very point. And although the difficulties are very much greater, those who have, with enormous care and sympathy, translated the Epistle into many other languages have found a similar response. The British and the American Bible societies have an impressive record of the relevance of the New Testament Epistles to life as people of very different backgrounds and cultures have to live it today.

Faith

As I WRITE these words I am aware of various things through my physical senses. As it happens, at the moment these are chiefly the light and warmth of sunshine, the beauty of trees in full leaf, the varied songs of birds and the distant sound of children at play. I am also mentally aware of the truth I am trying to express, and of you, my imaginary reader, following the line of thought I am trying to make clear. Doubtless as you read you are taking in similar sense impressions, as well as having your thoughts guided by the complicated system of marks made upon paper which we call printing. But simultaneously, in the immediate world of you the reader and me the writer, there are radio programs of various kinds actually in our rooms with us. The "ether" (for that is the name given to this all-pervasive but intangible medium) is continually pulsing and vibrating, strongly or feebly, with perhaps a hundred or more near or distant radio transmissions. In common parlance we frequently say that a certain program is "on the air"; but that, of course, is quite inaccurate. Radio transmissions are not vibrations in the air. They would function just as well if there were no air at all, and they make their way, as we all know, with very little hindrance through such things as timber, stone, and concrete. It is only when they meet conductors or partial conductors of electricity that these inaudible, invisible vibrations become minute electrical currents and even then they are undetectable except by that commonplace but quite complicated piece of circuitry known as a radio set. In your body, as in my body, there are at this very moment minute electrical currents of which we are quite unaware. They are, in fact, an untuned jumble of electrical vibrations representing the assorted offerings of many radio transmissions. Now we are unaware of this and normally we take no notice of it. It is only when we want to hear a particular radio program that we tune in a certain band of these etheric vibrations and by means of the radio set turn them back into audible sound. For even if we disapprove of radio, even if we refuse to believe in its all-pervasive presence, it makes not the slightest difference to the *fact*. Whether we like it or not, or whether we believe it or not, we are permeated by this mysterious "ether," and that is a fact which can easily be demonstrated. Before the advent of radio less than a century ago, such an idea would have seemed in the highest degree improbable and even impossible. We know today that it is true, that simultaneously with our ordinary-world sense impressions there co-exists a world of mysterious "ether" of which we only become aware when certain apparatus is used.

Now, this seems to me a most helpful, if simple, analogy. Suppose it is possible that the whole material world and the whole psychological world are interpenetrated by what we may call the "spiritual." For some reason or other we are inclined to think of the physical world and even the demonstrable world of the "ether" as somehow real, while the "spiritual" is regarded as unreal and imaginary. I believe the opposite to be true. As Paul foresaw long ago, "The things which are seen are temporal; but the things which are not seen are eternal" (2 Corinthians 4:18). Suppose what we are seeing and measuring and observing are the outward expressions in the time and space setup of what is really eternal and spiritual! If we make such a supposition we are in for a revolution in our whole way of thinking. But New Testament Christians had already experienced this revolution.

To sense the reality of the God-dimension, to conform to its purpose and order, to perceive its working in and through the visible world system is, speaking broadly, what the Bible calls faith.

Faith in the New Testament

IN THE GOSPELS it would appear in general that the existence and use of [the faculty of faith] provided the link between the Divine Order and human life. The centurion who earned Jesus' commendation for his "faith" plainly took it as a matter of course that as he occupied a position of authority in the purely earthly realm, so Jesus was able to exercise authority in the unseen realm (Matthew 8:5; Luke 7:2). It was not so much personal admiration for Jesus, and probably not full recognition of Who he really was, so much as an intuitive perception that here was One Who was a Master over the unseen forces which influence observed life. His "faith" was nevertheless a sincere recognition that there was a Divine Order which was real and reliable. Again, in the case of those four young men who were prepared to take desperate measures to get their friend to Jesus, there was the same recognition of the unseen Divine Order and Power (Mark 2:3; Luke 5:18). In both these cases, and of course in many others, the use of the faith faculty was, so to speak, the agent which enabled Jesus' power to be released. The contrary was also true. Where men were imprisoned by the closed system and could not, for reasons of prejudice or sheer unwillingness to believe, break through into the real dimensions, even the power of Jesus was inhibited. In Nazareth, "He could do no mighty works there because of their unbelief" (Matthew 13:58). We read moreover that "he marveled because of their unbelief" (Mark 6:4), and surely we may fairly guess that his observation of men's failure to use their faculty of faith must have continually astonished him. To him the Unseen Dimension and Order were continuously real. The love, the generosity, and the power of the Father were constant realities, and it must not only have amazed but grieved him more than we can guess to find men either unwilling or unable to use the power of faith. Again and again, he urges men to "have faith in God," and both by his own teaching and his own example it is plain that he is continually urging men to put the weight of their confidence not in earthly schemes and values, but in the unseen Heavenly Order, of which the supreme Head is the Father. To live like this, to live as though the spiritual realities were infinitely more important than the appearance of things, might fairly be said to be a basic teaching of Jesus. To live "by faith" is to him the truly natural way of living, and although it may demand effort and persistence he does not hold it out as a way of living merely for the spiritual elite. It is only in the exceptional case, as in the case of the healing of the epileptic boy (Luke 9:39) that Jesus declares that training and discipline are necessary for faith to produce the requisite power for good. In general throughout the Gospels Jesus seems to be urging men to dare to use their faith faculty—to knock, to seek, to ask. His general implication is that there are boundless resources in the Unseen World available for men of faith.

Faith in the Young Church

WHEN WE COME to the book of the Acts of the Apostles or the letters of the New Testament, we are reading about what actually happened when men and women began to "believe in the Lord Jesus Christ." The burden of preaching in the Acts is not, so far as can be discovered, the emphasis on man's depravity, but on faith—the grasping by the faith faculty of the new order. Naturally, the focal point of this new apprehension is God's personal focusing of Himself in the Man Jesus Christ. The word translated "repentance" does not necessarily mean being sorry for our sins, though that will probably be included. *Metanoia* means a fundamental change of outlook. As far as we can discover in the early preaching of the Gospel, the Good News was not primarily the announcement of the fact that men were sinners, but that the real world had broken through into this world in visible, tangible form—in fact, in Christ. God was now knowable; His Plan of a universal Kingdom was manifest; death itself was of no account now that God had revealed Himself in Jesus. Simultaneously with this proclamation of Good News to Jews and Gentiles was the announcement that the living contemporary Spirit of God was alive and active. We have only to read the book of the Acts to see how He, the Holy Spirit, the Spirit of Jesus, empowered, transformed, and guided the early Christians. The Young Church was full of divine energy and wisdom; and it would seem that its members were so filled because they learned more and more to use the faculty of faith, and because they prayed, not indeed to persuade an unwilling

God, but to bring themselves into line with His Purpose so that the power could safely be given. No one could honestly read the book of the Acts with an adult mind without being impressed with this sense of suprahuman power, wisdom, and authority. God Himself is plainly at work in and through these new Christians who, for all their faults, were plainly exercising the faith faculty.

When we enter the world of the Letters, which reflect the life of the early Church, we are again faced with the phenomenon of people whose whole outlook and pattern of life are being transformed by the use of the same faculty of faith. If we examine even the letter of James, which is supposed to concern itself much more with "good works" than with "faith," we find on examination that the letter is merely a corrective against false ideas of what "faith" implies. "Of what use is it," says James in effect, "if you do see the unseen realities of God, His Kingdom, and His Order, unless that perception is expressed and worked out in ordinary human situations?" That is a very proper question, and it is part of the discipline of life that, although we may have our glimpses of the glory of God, though we may by faith thoroughly accept the truth of the "Incarnation," the "Atonement," and "Resurrection," and so on, all these shining revolutionary truths have to be expressed and worked out in the dust and darkness, even in the strain and squalor of the sinful human situation. Far from decrying the value of faith, James is concerned to prevent such a faculty from becoming romantically airborne. He is determined, and rightly determined, that just as the young Prince of Glory lived His matchless life in the dust and sweat of the human arena, so users of the faith faculty must not consider themselves above their Lord.

It is, of course, when we come to the Letters of Paul that we find the word "faith" used again and again. It is used in slightly different senses . . . but always it includes this idea of grasping a reality, a whole dimension of reality which we cannot see with our fleshly senses. Paul indeed draws the strong contrast between the man whose vision and outlook is limited to this world and the man who, by the action of the Spirit, becomes alive to spiritual realities.

Justification by Faith

ONE OF Paul's most important teachings, though it is only one, is the doctrine of what we call "justification by faith." It frequently appears to the non-Christian mind that this is an immoral or at least unmoral doctrine. Paul appears to be saying that a man is justified before God not by his goodness or badness, not by his good deeds or bad deeds, but by believing in a certain doctrine of the Atonement.

Of course, when we come to examine the matter more closely we can see that there is nothing unmoral in this teaching at all. For if "faith" means using a God-given faculty to apprehend the unseen divine order, and means, moreover, involving oneself in that order by personal commitment, we can at once see how different that is from merely accepting a certain view of Christian redemption. What Paul is concerned to point out again and again is that no man can reconcile himself to the moral perfection of God by his own efforts in this time-and-space setup. It is a foregone conclusion that he must fail. The truth is—and of course it is a truth which can only be seen and accepted by the faith faculty—that God has taken the initiative, that, staggering as it may seem, one of the main objects of the Personal Visit was to reconcile man to Himself. That which man in every religion, every century, every country, was powerless to effect, God has achieved by the devastating humility of His action and suffering in Jesus Christ. Now, accepting such an action as a *fait accompli* is only possible by this perspective faculty of "faith." It requires not merely intellectual assent but a shifting of personal trust from the achievements of the self to the completely undeserved action of God. To accept this teaching by mind and heart does indeed require a *metanoia*, a revolution in the outlook of both mind and heart. Although the natural human personality sometimes regards this generous fact of reconciliation as an affront to its pride, to countless people since Paul's day it has been, as it was meant to be, Good News.

The phrase "justification by faith," then, simply means acceptance of a forgiveness and a reconciliation made by God Himself, and the total abandonment of efforts at self-justification. God's action, His "grace," as Paul calls it, becomes effectual when the truth of the matter becomes real by "faith." That is why Paul repeats again and again in different words his great theme, "By grace are ye saved through faith; and that not of yourselves: it is the gift of God" (Ephesians 2:8).

Faith in Today's World

IF WE ARE genuinely willing to welcome the fresh wind of the Spirit and to experience once again the God-given vigor of the early Church, we must plainly begin by reusing the faculty of faith. Perhaps it would be not out of place here to make a few suggestions which for convenience sake may be numbered:

(1) Let us deliberately take time to consider our modern situation, not so much its problems but its attitude of mind

and spirit. A few chapters read from the Acts of the Apostles might help us to appreciate by contrast how closed we have grown on the God-ward side. Perhaps we might, with as fresh minds as we can, read some of the Gospel incidents as well so that we may become convinced afresh that the fault in our present-day Christianity lies not in God with His astonishing generosity, but in our own neglected capacity to believe, to reach out and appropriate His resources. Although we are not responsible for our talents or lack of them, we are very largely responsible for our own attitude of mind. Let us without morbid self-accusing confess that we have largely neglected to use our God-given faculty of faith. Let us freely admit that at heart our life attitude has been a long way from that of men attuned to unseen realities.

(2) Let us by conscious and deliberate effort begin to exercise the long-disused faculty. Whatever our circumstances may be, life is so arranged that there is never a lack of opportunity for such exercise. It is apparent that, both for considering our own position in relation to God and for deliberately using our power of faith, we need a quiet space in our lives. This is absolutely essential, and nothing is more important than securing this space amid all our busyness. No one is too busy to set aside a period of, say, a quarter of an hour each day for such quiet. (We are all rather ridiculous here. For if we knew for certain that a space of a quarter of an hour's quiet was essential for our physical health, for example, we should unhesitatingly make room for it. It would become a top priority. Can we not see that such a period, which should be regarded as a minimum, could be absolutely essential for our spiritual health?) For many people this period of quiet must of necessity be solitary; but since a great deal of the vigor of the early Church depended on Christian fellowship and was in fact given and demonstrated through Christian fellowship, there is

good reason to suppose that a small God-seeking group of people might help one another enormously in redeveloping the faith faculty.

(3) Study of the New Testament with as unbiased and unprejudiced a mind as possible will undoubtedly stimulate faith itself and the desire to develop the faculty more. Before long we cannot help realizing, if we "soak" ourselves in the meaning and spirit of these inspired pages, that this other world, which we have been in the habit of regarding as shadowy and far away, can, and in fact historically did, permeate ordinary human life. Further, we shall conclude that there is no valid reason for supposing that if the right conditions are fulfilled the same suprahuman quality and power could not penetrate life today.

(4) Jesus told men "to knock," "to seek," and "to ask," by which I understand him to mean that although the resources of God are always available, it is up to us men to make use of them. I think, too, that he may well have meant men to make spiritual experiments, to try out, as it were, the Divine resources. As we do this, we shall inevitably find that the values and fortunes of this passing world become less important and clamant. Nevertheless, I think we should be wise, by deliberately training ourselves, to see that real security does not, indeed cannot, rest in this world, however lucky or careful we may be. Moreover, all experiences of love and beauty, much as we may enjoy and appreciate them in this transitory life, are not rooted here at all. We should save ourselves a lot of disillusionment and heartbreak if we reminded ourselves constantly that here we have "no continuing city" (Hebrews 13:14). The world is rich with all kinds of wonders and beauties, but we only doom ourselves to disappointment if we think that the stuff of this world is permanent: its change and decay are inevitable. The rich variety of transitory beauty is no more than a reflection or a foretaste of the real and the permanent.

Something surely of this thought is included in Christ's words, "Lay up for yourselves treasures in Heaven, where neither moth nor rust doth corrupt, and where thieves do not break through nor steal" (Matthew 6:20).

(5) Finally, we must accept as one of the facts of life that to live on this level and to retain this attitude of mind and heart are not as easy as falling off a log. Sometimes, it is true, to do so is easy and natural, but there are other times when contemporary pressures and even our own lethargy make it difficult to rise and live as sons and daughters of the Most High. We must cheerfully accept the fact that, cost what it may, for the time being "we walk by faith, not by sight" (2 Corinthians 5:7). To exercise faith will often mean an effort on our part, a determined breaking through of the matted layers of this world's self-sufficiency, and a persistent reaching out to touch the living God.

Hope

HOPE RUNS HIGH in the inspired pages; it is not a superior form of pious wishful thinking but hope based solidly upon the character and purpose of God Himself. But for us, during the last fifty years particularly, the quality of hope has ebbed away from our common life almost imperceptibly. I say again that we are affected far more than we know, far more than we should be, by the prevailing atmosphere of thought around us. Christians, at any rate as far as western Europe is concerned, do not seem to exhibit much more hope than their non-Christian contemporaries. There is an unacknowledged and unexpressed fear in the hearts of many people that somehow the world has slipped beyond the control of God. Their reason may tell them that this cannot be so, but the constant assault of world tensions and the ever present threat of annihilation by nuclear weapons make people feel that the present setup is so radically different that the old rules no longer apply. Without realizing it, many of us are beginning to consent in our inmost hearts to the conclusion that we live in a hopeless situation. . . .

A very great deal of what passes for hope today is either wishful expectation or the expressed reaction of a mind which is not prepared to face realities. We shall not find in the New Testament, I think, a single instance of hope used in any but its genuine sense, that is, hope rooted in the good Purpose of God. You will remember how James in his New Testament letter is particularly severe in his condemnation of the "pious hope" for other people's good which does nothing practical to implement the wish (James 2:15–16). He says in effect that if you should see people cold or hungry or without proper clothes, and you say, "Well, God bless you—I hope you will soon be all right!" what on earth is the good of that? This sort of pious hope is still with us. People will say, for example, "I do hope they will soon find a cure for cancer," but many of them would not dream of giving a penny to any anticancer research fund. Or they will say, "I do hope something is done for all those thousands and thousands of poor refugees and homeless people over there in Europe." But not one in a hundred who expresses such a hope does anything to make it come true. We have to rid our minds of both pious hopes and wishful thinking before we get down to solid, genuine hope.

Hope in the New Testament and the Young Church

THE INSPIRED WRITINGS of the New Testament are neither optimistic nor pessimistic; they are very far from being the enthusiastic outpourings of people expressing their ideals and painting rosy pictures of a dream world which might one day be true. Nor, on the other hand, do the writers underline the sinfulness and depravity of human nature. We are reading what was written by men at firsthand grips with realities, and it is both astonishing and heartening to find how hopeful they are. Unless we happen to have studied ancient history, we may not have realized how remarkable are the bright hopes of the early band of Christians. The surrounding pagan world was dark; it was full of fear, cruelty, and superstition. For the most part the old religions had failed. Human life had become cheap; common morality was in many cases very lightly regarded; and belief in a world to come was almost nonexistent. . . . But in the Young Church there was gay and indomitable hope. Nothing could quench this hope, for these men and women now knew through Christ what God was like, and they now knew for certain that death was a defeated enemy. While the pagan world had largely become sodden with self-indulgence and ridden by the fear of death, the brave new fellowship of believers in Christ was a light and a flame in the darkness; it was a fellowship of hope.

All hope in the New Testament . . . rests upon the Nature and Purpose of God. These men and women are hopeful because, as Jesus Christ told men, "with God all things are possible" (Mark 10:27). Those who had come to believe with complete conviction that God loves the world, that He has visited it in Person and shown His power in transforming the lives of the most unlikely characters, were not readily disposed to lose hope in His ultimate Purpose. But of course that hope was not limited to the present temporary scene that we call life. The center of gravity of their hope was in the eternal and not in the temporal world. This was the quality which both baffled and infuriated their enemies as fierce persecution began to arise. The pagan world with its ever present horror of death could scarcely believe the evidence of their senses when they found in the Christian martyrs men and women to whom death was not a disaster at all. To the pagan mind to take a man's life was to take his all, but to attack Christians by sword, torture, or the atrocities of the arena was to invite defeat. Even if you killed them they slipped through your fingers to be with their Lord forever!

Although New Testament Christians doubtless prayed, as we do, "Thy Kingdom come, Thy Will be done on Earth, as it is in Heaven," and though they therefore doubtless worked and prayed for the improvement of the world in which they lived, their hope rested upon God, not merely upon what He could do in this world, but upon His high, mysterious Purpose. Of comparatively recent years the center of our faith has become, at any rate in some quarters, more and more earthbound. We are concerned with the Christian attitude to housing, to social problems, to juvenile delinquency, to international relationships, and indeed to every department of human life. This is fine as far as it goes, but sometimes one gets the impression that Christians are "falling over backwards" to disavow their otherworldliness. Yet to have the soul firmly anchored in Heaven rather than grounded in this little sphere is far more like New Testament Christianity.

Hope in Today's World

IT IS ESSENTIAL that we recapture and hold fast the New Testament idea that God is the "God of hope" (Romans 15:13). In the New Testament writings there is a continual sense not only of the immediacy but of the contemporaneousness of God. Their authors can write realistically of the God of hope because they are very close in point of time to God's act of intervention in what nowadays we call the Incarnation, and because the power of the Young Church is very plainly and demonstrably the power of the living Spirit. Many modern Christians are inclined to put God back into the past. How many times in visiting various churches does one hear of what used to happen in the old days! And, since Christians derive a great deal of their inspiration from reading the Bible, they can all too easily envisage God as thoroughly at home in the sacred pages but somehow no part of the modern picture at all. In [*New Testament Christianity*] I recalled how I tested a group of young people by asking them to give a quick answer to the question "Do you think God understands radar?" And how the answer was "No," to be followed of course by laughter as the absurdity became apparent. But I am still convinced that the unpremeditated answer was highly significant and revealing. Without admitting it in so many words, many Christians today cannot readily conceive of God operating in a world of television, washing machines, atomic fission, automation, psychiatry, electronic brains, glossy magazines, modern music, and jet propulsion. The complication and speed of present-day living make it extremely difficult for the mind to imagine the Biblical God interpenetrating such a system and operating within its pressures. The very word "God" seems out of key and even bizarre in our modern context.

Two things are necessary if we are to rediscover the buoyant hope of the New Testament. The first obvious step is to make certain that our hope is really hope and not either wishful thinking or merely pious hope. It must be closely allied to our faith and must ultimately be rooted in what we know for certain of the Nature and Purpose of God Himself. We might do well to study afresh the kind of hopes which sustained and inspired the Young Church and compare them with our own. This will naturally bring us to our next step, which is to rediscover the contemporaneousness of God. This may require a drastic revolution in our thinking, for we may discover that we have been thinking of God as Someone we can escape to, rather than Someone Who is actually not only in ourselves but in the noisy hurly-burly of everyday life. This does not mean to deny that modern life is distracting, complex, and difficult, but it does mean realizing afresh that God is not in the slightest degree baffled or bewildered by what baffles and bewilders us. It is no good longing for the monastic quiet of a past age or for the simplicity of life of a pastoral generation. Our urgent need is to discover God, the God of hope, in the present strain, in the complex problem, actually at work in the given situation. For He is either a present help or He is not much help at all.

The Love Commandments

To LOVE God with the whole of our personalities and powers is, according to the words of Christ recorded in Matthew
22:38, the "first and great commandment." Yet among the
thousands of people outside the ranks of the Church there
would be very few who could be found to agree with him.
"Be a decent chap and don't worry your head too much
about God"—this is the working philosophy of a good
many people.

Those of us who profess and call ourselves Christians are
committed to accept Christ's authority, though not unthink-
ingly; and when we come to look behind what appear at
first to be arbitrary commands, we find that invariably He
had good reasons for the principles He laid down. So it is
here. . . .

Unless we believe in God and love Him, the qualities we
value, the things we call "good" or "bad," are purely a matter of personal opinion. Your "good" may be my "bad" and
vice versa. . . . But Christians have an influence on national thought and conscience out of all proportion to their
numerical strength; and even today a very large part of our
tradition of behavior is nothing less than the fruit of Christian ideals having percolated almost imperceptibly into our
habits of thinking. . . .

It is comparatively easy for us to love those "neighbors"
who are nice and friendly towards us. It is easy to love the
attractive and charming personalities of our friends. But
Christ made it quite clear that loving our "neighbor" did
not stop at loving our particular circle, but loving all those
with whom life brought us into contact.

You will remember His semi-humorous comment on those who thought that to love their particular friends was enough—"Do not even the publicans the same?" We might paraphrase that—"Aren't even the tax-collectors nice to their pals?" No, if there is ever to be a happy and peaceful world we have all of us got to learn to understand and to love the difficult, the exasperating, and the unlovable—and that is a superhuman task.

I use the word "superhuman" deliberately, for by ourselves, without the inspiration that comes from loving God, it is plainly impossible for us to love, in the sense that Christ uses the word, our fellow men.

A clergyman probably realizes this far more acutely than the average layman. There are many departments of life where obviously you possess more knowledge and experience than I do; but in this matter of living in love and charity with all kinds of people the parson has to know a good deal. Forgive my plain speaking, but is it not true that if you find someone who is "difficult" or conceited or annoying, it is quite the easiest thing in the world for you simply to withdraw yourself and make friends with just those with whom you get on? But such a course is not open to me. I have to learn to understand and work with all kinds of different temperaments and outlooks, and in consequence I get a unique opportunity of seeing just how difficult is Christ's second commandment—to love other people as we love ourselves.

Frankly, I see no prospect of our even wanting to obey the second commandment seriously until we have begun to obey the first. We don't really see other men and women as our brothers and sisters simply by talking airily about the brotherhood of man. We only see them as such when we begin to get a vision of God the Father. It is so fatally easy to talk highfalutin hot air about all the world being "one big family," and yet fail to "get on" with the members of our own families, or with those who live next door, or in the [apartment] above us. In sober fact, men do not really love their fellows, except their own particular friends, until they have seriously begun to love God. It is only then that we learn to drop the destructive attitude of hatred and contempt and criticism, and begin to adopt the constructive attitude of Christian love. So, then, the second reason for the command to love God being "the first and great commandment" is that we don't really keep the second until we have obeyed the first.

Love in the New Testament and the Young Church

"GOD" IN VARIOUS religions might be thought of as benevolent toward the mortal creation, but the reason that the Gospel was Good News when it first burst upon the world was simply that men had realized that God is Love. The revelation of character provided by Christ Himself, the awe-full brunt of suffering which He was prepared to bear in order to redeem mankind, His triumph over man's last enemy, His ascension to timeless reality, taking Human Nature with Him as it were; His continual coming by the Spirit to transform and reinforce men's lives—all these, the unshakable conviction of the Young Church, showed one thing: that God is by nature Love and that He loves mankind. Men who accepted this foundation truth found an indefinable endorsement of it in their own hearts. They also found that their own "love-energy," which had previously been turned in upon themselves or was being given to the wrong things, now became an outflowing love embracing their fellow men for whom Christ died. Further, this love not only changed in direction but in quality. It was something more than natural love; it began to resemble Divine Love. Indeed, it is hardly an exaggeration to say that Christianity gave the word "love" a new and deeper meaning. The new love was stimulated and developed by accepting the love of God as shown in Christ. "If God then so loved us we ought also to love our brethren," wrote John (1 John 4:11). The new life of faith and hope is made possible, according to Paul, "because the love of God is shed abroad in our hearts" (Romans 5:5).

I am quite sure that a great deal of the joyful experience and invincible courage of the Young Church is due simply to the fact that the early Christians believed these words to be literally true. To them nothing could alter this basic fact, and no experience of life could separate them from God's unremitting love.

Four Temptations Against Love

ALL THOSE WHO try to love are beset by certain temptations of which these are the chief:

(1) *The temptation to imitate love.* . . . It is perfectly possible for us to behave kindly, justly, and correctly toward one another and yet withhold that giving of the "self" which is the essence of love. Married people will perhaps more easily appreciate what I am trying to say. A husband may behave with perfect kindness and consideration toward his wife; he may give her a generous allowance; he may do more than

his share of the household chores, and indeed he may do all the things which an ideal husband is supposed to do. But if he withholds "himself" the marriage will be impoverished. Women who seem to know these things intuitively would infinitely prefer the husband to be less kind, considerate, and self-sacrificing if they were only sure that he with all his imperfections and maddening ways gave "himself" in love in the marriage. This principle applies to some extent to all human relationships, and I am quite certain that it is this costly, self-giving love which Paul had in mind in 1 Corinthians 13. Many, even among Christians, shrink from it, not I think because they are afraid to give but because they are afraid that their gift will not be appreciated; in short, that they may be hurt. But surely this is the risk that love must always take, and without this giving of the self with all the risks that that entails, love is a poor pale imitation. "Consider *him*" (Hebrews 12:3) writes the author of the Epistle to the Hebrews, and if we do we find this is precisely the sort of rejectable, vulnerable love Christ lived and died to prove.

(2) *The temptation to hate oneself.* The cheerful pagan takes himself as a rule very much for granted, but the Christian who is sooner or later brought face to face with Truth is disgusted and dispirited to find how self-loving and self-centered his life really is. The more he comes into contact with the living Christ, the more he realizes there is to be put right, and if he is not careful his normal pride and self-respect go suddenly "into reverse." The more he thinks of the standards of love and those who live by them, the more wrong he feels, until he ends with a thoroughgoing contempt for himself and all his doings. The self with whom he has lived for some years in reasonable comfort becomes an intolerable person; before long he has slipped into despising himself wholeheartedly. Now this, despite what some

religious books have said, is a thoroughly bad state of mind in which to live. The man who despises or hates himself will sooner or later, despite all his religious protestations, reveal hatred and contempt for his brother men. Whatever his profession of love for "sinners," the contempt for the sin which he has found in himself is all too easily projected onto those who sin.

(3) *The temptation to separate love of God from love of people.* "The more I see of some people, the more I love my dog," runs the modern half-humorous comment. Of course, it is far easier to love a devoted animal who more than rewards us by the utmost fidelity and affection than it is to love people who in addition to being much more complex beings often do not reward us at all. Similarly, it is easy to love humanity without loving people. Many of the greatest crimes against individual living people have been committed in the name of love for humanity. There are plenty of people with us today who will talk about world peace and the universal brotherhood of man but who cannot get on with their own families or neighbors. People, in fact, unless they happen to be our own special friends, are quite difficult to love.

Naturally, Jesus knew this very well and he connected inseparably the love of God with the love of other people. Indeed, it is part of the act of Incarnation that God and human beings are indissolubly wedded. This is the kind of fact which most of us would rather not have to face. It is comparatively easy for us to imagine God as the Perfection of all beauty, truth, and love and to respond with worship and adoration to such a Being. What we find almost too much to stomach is that this very same God has allied Himself through Christ with ordinary human beings. In Jesus' famous parable of the Last Judgment (Matthew 25:31–46), men find to their astonishment that their treatment of fellow human beings is adjudged to be the same thing as their treatment of Christ Himself. . . .

(4) *The temptation to feel that people are not worth loving.* The world is lamentably short of outgoing love. Part of the reason for this is that it is so much easier to love among our own circle or at least to love those who will return our love. Although we do not express it in so many words, I believe that one of the reasons so few people venture to give themselves for the sake of other people is that they feel that "people are not really worth it." But who are we, who call ourselves Christians, "saved," pillars of the Church, and so on? In what way do we think that we were "worth it," when Christ visited this earth to save us? In the eyes of Heaven this whole sin-infected, blundering human race could hardly have seemed worthy of the highest sacrifice which God Himself could make for its redemption. Yet Love took the initiative and bore unspeakable contradiction, misunderstanding, and humiliation to win us to Himself. To quote John's words again, "If God so loved us, we ought also to love one another" (1 John 4:11).

Love in Today's World

"THE GREATEST OF these is love" (1 Corinthians 13:13), wrote Paul long ago, and we all agree, with admiration. But how far do our lives endorse what we assent to so readily? "The greatest of these is success" might well be the motto of many people, even though they themselves are not successful. "The greatest of these is security" is the motto of countless thousands. "The greatest of these is knowledge" is the unexpressed opinion of many of our scientifically-minded generation. We have to become convinced afresh that Paul's inspired words are quite literally true. Love is the greatest because without it there is no worthwhile success and certainly no real security. Love is the greatest because men are never transformed at heart permanently except by love. Love is the greatest because without it knowledge can become dangerous and even suicidal. Above all, love is the greatest because it persists beyond the confines of this temporal existence. The success of the film star, the brilliance of the best-selling novelist, the speed of the record-breaking athlete, the awe-inspiring knowledge of the top-secret scientist—of what value will these and a hundred other highly prized worldly achievements amount to in the Real World to which we are bound? But what has been done in love—the problems that have been solved, the personalities redeemed, the situations changed, the actual growth of character beneath the influence of love—all these will stand as permanent and demonstrable evidence of the Divine Purpose of Life. All of us are inclined to be swayed more than we realize by the values of the world in which we live, but must we be so dazzled and blinded that we fail to see the paramount importance as well as the permanence of Love?

Peace

DESPITE THE FIRE, energy, daring, hope, and faith that distinguished the Young Church, there is no trace of hysteria or morbid excitement in its recorded life. Some of us have seen people do all sorts of extraordinary things under the influence of religious excitement, and those of us who are pastors of souls have sometimes been not a little perturbed at the dangers of arousing religious emotions and at their equally dangerous reactions. But as we study New Testament Christianity we are aware that there is an inner core of tranquility and stability. In fact, not the least of the impressive qualities which the Church could demonstrate to the pagan world was this ballast of inward peace. It was, I think, something new that was appearing in the lives of human beings. It was not mere absence of strife or conflict, and certainly not the absence of what ordinarily makes for anxiety; nor was it a lack of sensitivity or a complacent self-satisfaction, which can often produce an apparent tranquility of spirit. It was a positive peace, a solid foundation which held fast amid all the turmoil of human experience. It was, in short, the experience of Christ's bequest when He said, "Peace I leave with you, my peace I give unto you: not as the world giveth, give I unto you" (John 14:27).

Although essential human nature has not changed, outward circumstances have changed enormously since the early days of the Christian faith. I do not think that we can claim that life is either more difficult or more dangerous, but modern living is certainly more complex and is certainly conducted at a higher speed. The natural factors which tend to destroy peace and tranquility are greater than ever. All the more reason, then, for Christians to experience and, consciously or unconsciously, to show living evidence of the divine gift—of the unshakable inner core of peace.

"Peace with God" is sometimes rather carelessly used in religious circles as though it had only one connotation, as though all the problems of a complex human personality were solved if only a man would accept the redemptive sacrifice of Christ upon the Cross. Actually, this is an oversimplification, for although to accept the reconciliation which God has provided is an absolute essential, there are many other factors, especially among the more intelligent, which prevent the soul from being at peace. The divine peace, the steady centering of life upon God, is basically a gift from God and must be accepted, like our forgiveness, as His gift and not as something that we can achieve. Nevertheless there are elements within our own personalities which must be frankly faced before we can expect to experience that gift. If we want to enjoy inward tranquility amid this whirling, bewildering modern life, we must be prepared to do some honest self-examination. In the last resort we shall find that our only true peace is "peace with God," but it may not prove quite so simple to find it as we imagined.

Six Obstacles to Peace

(1) *Self-indulgence.* In all of us, to a greater or less degree, depending on heredity, upbringing, and temperament, there is a thrusting, self-pleasing element which normally regards the world as centering upon oneself. It is not a thing to be horrified at, for it is in us all, but the whole way of thinking and feeling which belongs to the self-centered man must be abrogated or denied before there can be peace with God. What we call "sins" are simply expressions of this self-pleasing, self-regarding, and self-indulgent inward attitude. The word which is translated in the New Testament as "repentance" really means a thorough change of heart and mind. It means realizing that the real center of everything is not my little self, but God, and that in order to serve the King Himself, I must quit the throne of my own precious little kingdom. To some people this comes easily,

almost naturally, as soon as they see the truth of it. To others it means a hard and even agonizing struggle. Such people do not readily surrender; they do not easily cooperate with someone else's plan, even if that Someone Else is God. Yet it is obvious that there can be no inward peace until the self-conscious inward kingdom willingly and wholeheartedly concedes its rights to the Creator, the real King. . . .

(2) *Inner conflicts and tensions.* If we are quiet before God and allow His Spirit to shine upon our inward state, we shall probably discover more than one conflict which is robbing us of inner peace. The man who lives apart from God may be largely unconscious of his inward conflicts and only aware of their tension. Of course, he may be driven by the sheer force of the tension to a psychiatrist who, if he is a wise one, will help the man to realize the sources of his disharmony. But he still will not be at peace with the Nature of things, with his own conscience and the Divine Purpose that is being worked out in this world, unless the psychiatrist is able to lead him to faith in God. But except in unusual cases, the Christian need not turn to the psychiatrist. Either alone with God or with the help of a trusted friend, priest, or minister, he can, if he wishes, see for himself the fierce hidden resentment, the carefully concealed self-importance, the obstinate and unforgiving spirit, and all the other things which prevent inward relaxation. As long as his personality is a battleground it is foolish to suggest to him that he accept the peace of God. His hidden desires, ambitions, and pride must first be brought to the surface, not only to the surface of his own consciousness but, as it were, to the light of God's love and understanding. God is not concerned to condemn; however ashamed and guilty the man himself may feel, God is concerned to heal and to harmonize.

(3) *Reluctance to pray for peace.* For sheer practical wis-

dom Paul's famous words have never been surpassed. He wrote: "Be careful for nothing; but in every thing by prayer and supplication with thanksgiving let your requests be made known unto God. And the peace of God, which passeth all understanding, shall keep your hearts and minds through Christ Jesus" (Philippians 4:6–7). It is when the love of God is allowed to penetrate every corner of a man's being that the peace of God comes as a positive gift, as a sturdy guardian of the soul's inward rest. The sharing of anxieties and fears, the intimate thankfulness for joys and beauties, bring the individual very close to the life of God. They must be habitual and they must be practiced, but their fruit is a relaxed spirit.

(4) *Fear of inadequacy.* Much of our tension and anxiety can be traced directly to a fear of inadequacy. We should meet this fear in two ways. First, by learning to accept ourselves. We probably are *not* adequate for all our ambitious schemes, and only at the cost of enormous nervous energy can we succeed in becoming momentarily what we really are not. This is a self-imposed tyranny which is very common. Suppose we accept ourselves good-humoredly, realizing our limitations and how much we have to learn, with cheerfulness and without envy of those who are, or appear to be, more adequate than ourselves. It is simply no use at all claiming the gift of God's peace if we are ridden by an overmastering desire to appear bigger or cleverer or more important than we really are. We must first learn to practice acceptance. The second step is to learn to accept life, as Jesus Himself did, at the Father's hands *day by day*. It was not a cynic but the Son of God Himself Who said, "One day's trouble is enough for one day" (Matthew 6:34). We are assured by many inspired promises that God will give us, as we require it, the ability to cope with life victoriously on this day-by-day basis. We must teach ourselves to get out of the habit of thinking too far ahead, of imagining our-

selves tomorrow or next week as inadequate for a situation which exists only in our minds. The sooner we can get it into our feverish souls that we are meant to live a day at a time, the more we shall be able to enjoy that sense of adequacy which spells peace of mind.

(5) *Peace cannot be earned.* I have mentioned above only a few of the psychological factors which may prevent us from enjoying the peace of God. To some simple natures it will appear as though I have overcomplicated the issue. But it is the fortunate few whose inward growth and life is so simple (and by that of course I do not mean stupid) that they can quite readily accept in unquestioning faith the peace of God within their hearts. To others it will naturally appear that I have done no more than touch upon their difficulties, which indeed is all that I have done. I can only recommend here that there must be a full, unashamed bringing to the surface of all the warring elements within the personality. In making such unravelings and adjustments as we can, we are not creating peace; we are only creating conditions for the coming of peace. When our hearts are possessed by this gift of God, we know for certain how true it is that it "passeth man's understanding." Outward circumstances may be tempestuous; common sense may tell us that it is absurd to be at peace under such a load or such a threat. But the gift is supranatural; it goes far beyond earthly common sense. It is, like faith, hope, and love, rooted in the Purpose of God.

(6) *Misalignment with God's purpose.* Peace with God is not a static emotion. It is a positive gift which accompanies our living in harmony with God's Plan. Dante's oft quoted saying, "And in His will is our peace," is not to be understood as surrender, resignation, and quiescence. The Christian will discover that he knows God's peace as he is aligned with God's Purpose. He may be called upon to be strenuous, but he is inwardly relaxed because he knows he

is doing the Will of God. This sense of knowing that he is cooperating with the Purpose defies human analysis and is always found singularly irritating by the opponent of Christianity. But Christians of all ages, not excepting our own, have found it to be true. However painful or difficult or, on the other hand, however inconspicuous or humdrum the life may be, the Christian finds his peace in accepting and playing his part in the Master Plan. Here again we must ask ourselves, "Am I doing what God wants me to do?" It is not a question of what my friends or a particular Christian pressure group want me to do, but of what God Himself wishes. By sharing our life with God, by throwing open our personality to His love and wisdom, we can know beyond any doubting what is God's will for us. When we are at one with Him in spirit and at one with Him in purpose, we may know the deep satisfaction of the peace of God.

Christian Maintenance

IN ORDER TO live a life of New Testament quality we shall find it necessary to work out some kind of practical plan to keep us alive and sensitive to the Spirit of the living God, which will keep us supplied day by day with the necessary spiritual reinforcement, and which will help us to grow and develop as sons and daughters of God. It is, unfortunately, only too easy to slip back into conformity with our immediate surroundings and to lose sight of the suprahuman way of living, except perhaps as a wistful memory. This does not in the least mean that real Christian living is a kind of spiritual tightrope walk, a fantastic and unnatural progress which can only be maintained by intense concentration. On the contrary, the Christian way of living is *real* living, and it carries all the satisfaction and exhilaration which living in reality can bring. It is quite simply because we are surrounded by unreal and false values, by a pattern of living divorced from and unconscious of spiritual realities, that we have to take time and trouble to maintain supranatural life, even though that life is in the truest sense the natural one. Experience shows that Christians whose lives are illuminated by the new quality of living only maintain that inner radiance by taking certain practical steps. Naturally, these will vary in individual cases, and there are people who, either by temperament or through long years of practice, can absorb God through the pores of their being, so to speak, as naturally and easily as most of us can breathe. But for the majority of us who are walking "by faith and not by sight" there are some essentials for the maintenance of real Christian living.

Quietude

THE HIGHER THE function of the human spirit, the more necessity for quietude. We cannot, for example, solve a difficult mathematical problem, neither can we appreciate good music, nor indeed art in any form, if we are surrounded by noisy distractions. It is imperative that somehow or other we make for ourselves a period of quiet each day. I know how difficult this is for many people in busy households, and for some even the bedroom is not quiet or private enough. But if we see the utter necessity for this period of quiet our ingenuity will find a way of securing it. Many churches are open for this purpose, among others, and there is no reason at all why we should not use the quiet of the reading room of the Public Library. But daily quiet we simply must secure, or the noise and pressure of modern life will quickly smother our longing to live life of the new quality.

What we must do in the period of quiet is to open our lives to God—to perfect understanding, wisdom and love. Perhaps it seems unnecessary to point this out, yet pastoral experience convinces me that people need to be reminded that we must be completely natural and uninhibited in our approach to the God "in Whom we live and move and have our being." Most practicing Christians have got beyond feeling that God must be addressed in Elizabethan English in deference to His Majesty, but there still lingers on an idea that we must be spiritually "dressed in our best" as we approach Him. I am far from suggesting that we should ever treat the awe-inspiring mystery of God with over-familiarity. Yet we know perfectly well, on the authority of Christ, that He is our heavenly Father, and our common sense tells us that, although He respects our individuality and our privacy, yet everything about us is quite open to His eyes. We are not addressing some superearthly King, some magnified Boss; we are not even addressing a purified and enlarged image of our own earthly fathers. We are opening our hearts and minds to Love, and we need have no fears, no reticences, and no pretenses. Strange as it undoubtedly is, He loves us as we are, and indeed we shall make no sort of progress unless we approach Him as we are.

Prayer

PRAYER HAS so many aspects that it requires much longer treatment than I can give it here, and I will only mention three which seem to be the most important.

The first is the value of worship. For myself I do not think worship can be forced, nor can I imagine that God wants it so to be. But if we make a habit of associating all that is good, true, lovely, and heartwarming in our ordinary experience of life and people with Him Who is the Source of every good and perfect gift; if without forcing ourselves to be grateful we quietly recount those things for which we can be truly thankful; if we allow our own dreams and aspirations to lead us upward to the One from Whom they are in fact derived, we shall not infrequently find that the springs of worship begin to flow. Sometimes a consideration of the Character of Christ as revealed in the Gospels, sometimes a consideration of the whole vast Plan for man's redemption, and sometimes a consideration of the immense complexity and wisdom revealed in a dozen different departments by the researches of science will move us to wonder, admiration, awe, and worship.

The second important point I should like to make is that in our prayers we should not merely confess our sins and failures to God, but claim from Him the opposite virtue. If we stress again and again our own particular failings, we tend to accentuate and even to perpetuate them. Many of us Christians need to adopt a more positive attitude. We need to dare to draw upon the inexhaustible riches of Christ, not as though that were some poetic and metaphorical expression, but as though it were a fact. The Gospel is not Good News if it simply underlines our own sinfulness. That is either a foregone conclusion or it is Bad News! But the whole wonder and glory of the Gospel is that into people who have sinned and failed badly God can pour not only the healing of forgiveness but the positive reactivating power of goodness. It is not the mere overcoming of a fault that we should seek from God, but such an overflowing gift of the opposite virtue that we are transformed. I cannot believe that the miracles of personality transformation, which undoubtedly occurred in such places as Corinth and Ephesus nineteen centuries ago, are beyond the power of God's activity today. We are altogether too timorous and tentative. Why should we not make bold and far-reaching demands upon the spiritual riches which are placed at our disposal?

Thirdly, I should like to stress the value of intercession for other people. I do not pretend to understand the mystery of intercession, though I am sure it is never an attempt to bend the will of a reluctant God to do something good in other people's lives. But somehow in the mysterious spiritual economy in which we live we are required to give love, sympathy, and understanding in our prayers for others, and this releases God's power of love in ways and at depths which would otherwise prove beyond our reach. I confess I stand amazed at the power of intercessory prayer, and not least at what I can only call the "celestial ingenuity" of God. He does not, as a rule, directly intervene; He assaults no man's personality, and He never interferes with the free will which He has given to men. Yet, working within these apparently paralyzing limitations, God's love, wisdom, and power are released and become operative in response to faithful intercessory prayer. It is all part of the high Purpose, and all true Christians are responsibly involved in such praying.

Liturgy

IN THE PALMY days when I enjoyed the services of two first-class curates and an excellent lay reader, there were times when I was able to attend services at my own church by slipping quietly into a back pew.

I did this, in the first instance, with a critical professional eye and ear, so that our worship might be of the best possible quality. But, rather to my surprise, I found myself aware of an almost indescribable feeling among the congregation, which I can only describe as a wistful hunger to know more of God.

In the parish of which I am speaking, I should say that very few went to church out of mere habit or duty, and certainly none went because it was "the thing to do" (it wasn't!).

These people came to worship and to pray, but most of all (or so was my strong feeling) to hear more and learn more of the love of God.

Like anyone else who cares for the souls of men, I was moved almost to tears by the quiet receptiveness of ordinary people in church. For in the house of God, they have temporarily laid aside mundane pressures and responsibilities. For the time being at least they are set free from the rat race of competition and from the need to keep up appearances.

In a sense they are naked and vulnerable. More than a little puzzled, sometimes more than a little battered by life's problems, they are seeking news about God.

It is monstrous for the preacher to offer such people a theological digest on the latest book on demythologizing the Gospels. Neither have they come to church to hear the preacher thundering against the sins of those who are not within earshot.

> They simply want to know about God.
> They want to hear the Good News.
> May they always be given it!

Worship

IF YOU ACCEPT the Christian view of God . . . I think you'll find your desire to worship Him will come along two main lines.

First you'll trace to their source all the things that make you admire and love and wonder. It doesn't matter whether it's the beauty of nature, the loveliness of music or poetry, the fascinating charms of childhood, the wonder of falling in love, or any other of the thousand things that move us so deeply. We shall get into the habit of connecting them up with God and probably say a quiet "thank you" for them.

Sometimes, when I've read a book that has really touched me, or seen a picture that has shown some fresh beauty to me, I've felt I'd give a lot to meet the author or the painter and say a personal "thank you." I'm pretty sure you often feel the same.

The other day, looking at some white lilac and thinking what a miracle of beauty it is, I said to myself, "I wish I could meet the one who designed that . . ." and then, quite suddenly, I realized what I was saying! *It was God, my Father and your Father!* And I don't mind telling that I worshiped the Supreme Artist who designed and made white lilac.

That's the sort of thing I mean. Once you accept Christ's

teaching that God is our Father, hundreds of lovely and "wonderfull" things in everyday life make you want to say how thrilled and grateful you are. You'll want to *worship*.

The second way in which you'll want to worship goes rather deeper. . . . When "the penny drops," as we say, when you actually *realize* what sort of Person God must be to come to this earth as a baby, and live and die to show how genuinely He loves us men; and when you realize, as well, that even at this moment God is in the here and now, actually suffering and struggling with us and in us, I'm pretty certain you'll feel "that's the kind of God I could love, that's the kind of God I want to worship."

If I think of God as a kind of Superarchitect who planned this amazing universe from stars to atoms, I feel a bit dazed and awed, but I don't think I particularly want to love Him. It's only when I see God coming in Person into the stream of human living, when I see Him loving and cheering and healing and inspiring people not only when He was on earth in Person 1900 years ago, but *today* whenever He's given the chance, that I feel I want to love and work for and worship Him.

Once you get it, once you realize that *all the time,* even when you broke the rules or did something that you're bitterly ashamed of now, He loved you and was only waiting for the chance to get into touch with you, I think you'll want to worship too.

Sacraments in Life

HERE . . . ARE THREE ordinary things which have very little meaning as physical actions but which may carry with them something far beyond their apparently trivial significance.

(1) Two lovers kiss. To the observer who knows neither of them, this may seem a commonplace, meaningless, or indeed rather vulgar gesture. But to the lovers themselves it may convey a meaning far beyond ordinary means of expression. (2) Two men who have long been at enmity finally shake hands in reconciliation. Again, to the observer the mere physical action is not worth noticing, but it may be full of the most profound significance, reaching out in time far beyond the few seconds of the handclasp. (3) We may take the clapping of hands as a token of love, admiration, or appreciation of some great deed or difficult accomplishment. To a stranger to this planet the batting of hands together would appear ridiculous and would convey absolutely nothing of the emotional state which this rather odd action is expressing.

Then we may consider, not actions, but *things* which become highly charged with emotion, though scientifically speaking they remain exactly the same. Here are three examples:

First, a wedding cake, which is in outward appearance and by every scientific measurement exactly the same cake as it was when it stood in the confectioner's window. But it is now a wedding cake, used and consumed at the wedding of two people much in love with each other. In one sense, the scientific sense, the cake is not changed, but in the sense of experience it is now Bill and Joan's wedding cake, and to the friends, near or far, who eat it, it is quite a different thing from the same cake in a shop window.

Or, let us look at this old armchair. To the eyes of the secondhand furniture dealer it is worth perhaps only a few dollars, but to the sons and daughters of the family it is "mother's armchair." It is not merely special, but actually sacred to them because of its hallowed associations.

Or, we may take a Purple Heart, worth as metal not more than a dollar, but to the parents of the man who died winning it worth something beyond price.

Here, we see, are ordinary inanimate things invested with a particular significance and sanctity because of their association with the love and sacrifice of human beings.

Moreover, there are in this bewildering world in which we find ourselves set, things which strike deep spiritual chords within us, which are not explainable in scientific or rational terms. Music can be analyzed into all its resonances, fundamental and harmonic, and its rhythm and pattern explained, but there has never been any explanation of the ways in which it can stir and haunt a human soul. The surge and thunder of the sea, the smell of wood smoke, the woods carpeted with bluebells and a hundred other things can touch and move our spirits in a way science is powerless to explain. It is as though there was another dimension, perhaps several other dimensions, to which our human spirits in some degree respond.

From such things we see that the commonplace may be invested with the highest and purest emotion, and that there are depths and heights in our spirits which may be touched by the simplest of natural phenomena. Then we may well begin to suspect that this physical world is in fact shot through and through with spiritual realities. The physical is plainly often necessary in order to experience or express the spiritual, and what we call the physical may only be the outcrop in time and space of what are eternal realities.

Then we may begin to see the necessity of the Word becoming flesh. For since we cannot appreciate goodness, truth, or beauty until they are embodied in a thing or a person or an action, neither can we properly know the supreme Reality, God, until he becomes a Man and lives among us.

Communion and Common Sense

THE ADVICE THAT Jesus gave was always sound and practical. Reading the Gospels will show us that so far from urging men to retire from this world and contemplate God, the point that Jesus was continually trying to make was that men should see that the Kingdom of God was in the here and now. He pointed out that our relationship with God was intimately bound up with our relationship with our fellow men—that we could not expect, for example, the forgiveness of God unless we were prepared to extend forgiveness to those who had wronged us. The commonsense instincts were to be trusted. *"If you then for all your evil know how to give good gifts . . . how much more? . . ."* Life in the here and now was in one sense of eternal significance, for He Himself had linked Himself indissolubly to the life of Man: He said, *"Inasmuch as ye did it not . . . ye did it not unto Me"* (Matthew 25:31–46).

It was always actual human behavior that mattered to Jesus, and never rosy religious dreams. The young man who hoped to be told what he could add to the pyramid of his spiritual accomplishment was told to sell all he possessed and follow Christ. The man who sought to settle the nice point as to who really was his neighbor was told in effect that whatever human being was in need was his neighbor. The woman who cried out sentimentally, *"How wonderful it must be to have been your mother!"* was told, *"Yes, but still more wonderful to hear the Word of God and keep it"* (Luke 11:27–28).

There is always in the life and teaching of Jesus Christ a

note of downright common sense, of practical human living. We cannot therefore believe that, in instituting this
great Sacrament of His own Body and Blood, He would for
one moment forget the burden of His teaching. Doubtless
. . . through this planned contact with Himself, there will
be times when the spirit of man rises above the earthly
things. But since this life is so constructed that we have
always to return to the humdrum, the unpleasant, the difficult, and the ugly, surely this Sacrament was not primarily
designed to enable us to take flight of the spirit. If it means,
as it surely must, union with Christ Himself, it cannot
avoid meaning sharing something of His outlook, His life,
His work, in the here and now, so that in the midst of the
mystery there will always be the keynote of common sense
and practicality.

The Living Tradition

ALTHOUGH WE HAVE in Holy Communion far more than a
tradition, because we have in it something which is alive in
itself, yet it has of course a value simply as a tradition, that
is, as something men consider worth passing on from generation to generation. But it is unique in that the other end
of it is, so to speak, *alive,* intimately joined to the very life
of the Son of God Himself. We may perhaps appreciate this
better if we compare this living tradition which we possess
with some dead relic which we might, but do not in fact,
possess. If, for example, we possessed the actual clothes
worn by Christ, a lock of His hair, a piece of furniture
which He had made while He worked as a carpenter, or
even the actual chalice used at the Last Supper, what should

we, in fact, have? A relic of enormous historical value, even a piece of solid visible evidence. We may be sure that there would be those who would go into a kind of reverent trance before such objects. But it is almost certain that, as happens with people being confronted with, shall we say, a pair of shoes worn by George Washington or a pen used by Mark Twain, the mind and attention and heart of the beholder would be drawn *toward the past*. Our eyes would inevitably be drawn backward toward the fact of Christ's earthly existence instead of forward to His living Presence today. . . . But we have infinitely more than this, for instead of dead relics, however authentic and well preserved, we have a living lifeline, stretching unbroken to Christ Himself. We have all the comfort and security that comes from historic tradition; but instead of being given the sad nostalgia of looking at an object and saying: "Look, how wonderful! This is what He touched then," we are given an evergreen memorial which says in effect, *"This is what He touches now."*

Eucharistic Fellowship

THE FELLOWSHIP TO which we are called in this strange and honoring and humbling gift of God is inescapably a fellowship of Love which may easily mean a fellowship of suffering. There is joy and strength, of course, in this holy food and drink, but it is also an inevitable joining of forces with the vast Scheme of reconciliation and redemption. Now, there is something in our natural selves that may well make us wary of such a contact. The man who in his heart intends to go on being selfish or proud, or who has already decided how far his Christian convictions should carry him, is probably obeying a sound instinct when he keeps away from this glorious but perilous Sacrament. For, if the truth be told, men are often willing to put their trust in a god who in the end must be triumphant, simply because they want to be on the winning side; but they are not nearly so ready to bear any part of the cost of that winning. Yet the fellowship of the broken bread and the poured-out wine can mean no less than that. . . .

All meals have a fellowship value: we know people better when they have come to tea with us, for example. The man of the world who says to his friends, "Come and have a drink with me," is obeying a deep human instinct for the sacramental, however crudely we may think he expresses it. But this particular fellowship is naturally of a deeper and more important kind. We must not for a moment belittle the value of ordinary human social intercourse, whether it be held in connection with the Church or not. But here Christ Himself is inviting us to experience and enjoy normal human fellowship at a much deeper level. Together we are satisfying a common spiritual need; together we are rededicating our lives to the service of Christ with all that that may imply. Together we are making use of this Christ-appointed contact and opportunity. The fellowship may not express itself in a hearty backslapping way, but it should surely be expressed in a renewed sense of family solidarity. We are meeting together at one of the deepest levels open to us as human beings.

Holy Communion is surely always falling short of its true purpose if it fails to produce some sense of solidarity with our fellow worshippers. It must never be regarded as a luxury for the devout; high and mysterious though it is, it is also the ordained place of deepest fellowship for those who are committed to the Way of Christ, ordinary, faulty, and imperfect though they are.

Spiritual Nutrition

WE ARE ALL familiar with the mystery of ordinary physical digestion. Indeed, like a good many commonplace happenings of this life, we are so familiar with it that we fail to see its wonder. A, B, and C sit round a breakfast table and from the same packet of cornflakes, the same bowl of sugar, and the same pitcher of milk they all break their fast. By a very complex process and, in the last resort, by a mystery which no one can explain, the inanimate matter eaten by A becomes part of A, rebuilding his tissues, or providing him with energy, or slowly adding to his weight. Exactly the same inanimate physical materials become by a similar process part of B or C. A may be redhaired, B may be blond, C may be completely bald, yet the taking of precisely similar quantities of food makes no alteration in their characteristics, but simply becomes part of the physical bodies of A, B, and C. This sort of thing has happened so many million times that we have forgotten that it is not only a highly complex process but a very mysterious one. Now, here in this holy Sacrament we are asked to believe a greater wonder—greater not so much in degree as in quality. We are in fact asked to believe that through the commonplace miracle of physical absorption and nutrition God Himself quickens and nourishes the spiritual life within us. We cannot help thinking at once of the words of Christ in St. John's Gospel: "Except ye eat my flesh and drink my blood, ye have no life in you" (John 6:53). The absorption of Christ into the human soul is an utter necessity if a human being is to remain a Christian at all.

These words spoken by Christ have an obviously wider application than to the Sacrament of Holy Communion. A man may absorb Christ through meditation and contemplation, through the opening of his spirit to the Holy Spirit, by his communion and prayer and worship in his own private room with the living Christ. And yet it is difficult to avoid the conclusion that though Christ was speaking in the broadest possible way of feeding on Himself, He did have in mind the concentrated absorption of Himself which He appointed in the Memorial Meal.

The Christ Within Us

THE RECOLLECTION OF God, the worship of God with mind as well as heart, sincere prayer and thanksgiving, will all help to maintain the vigor of the Christ-life within us. But for inner nourishment can there be anything more appropriate than the bread and wine which Christ Himself declared to be His own Body and Blood?

It is obvious that the Christian life can be maintained without Holy Communion at all. Indeed, it is so maintained, for example, by both the Quakers and by the Salvation Army. But it is surely not the normal, surely not the "Catholic" way (in its proper sense), in which the Spirit has led the Church through the centuries. A man may lead a happy and useful life with only one lung, or with part of his internal organs removed by surgery, but that is not the norm. Obviously it is possible for God to give His grace in a dozen different ways, but it is difficult to see why Christ instituted this particular means of spiritual nutrition unless it had a particular point and purpose for the vast army of

His future followers. Indeed, it is true to say from experience that Christians, unless they are prejudiced, or conditioned by their upbringing, are drawn intuitively toward Holy Communion. Their own natural spiritual hunger draws them instinctively toward the holy provision of the Lord's Table.

All Christians know with sorrow the difference between their high vocation and their everyday failures. All Christians recognize the need for the continual reinforcement of the good and timeless element within their personalities. Here in this Sacrament, under cover of what is ordinary, Christ is prepared to do the extraordinary—to infuse fresh life, to heal, to stimulate, to provide that health of soul which is one of the important meanings of "holiness."

All healing of the body is really accomplished by the *vis medicatrix naturae*, the healing force of nature. The most that medicine and surgery can do is to give this natural force a chance to overcome disease. As we all know very well, in the healthy body there is a host of minor ills which is overcome by the natural force of healing without recourse to doctor or medicine. Similarly the healthy and vigorous mind rejects the unwholesome and copes valiantly with the difficult. It is surely not unreasonable to suppose that there is a *vis medicatrix naturae* of the soul which is quite capable of dealing with the temptations, the sins, and the setbacks of the spiritual life. But only a healthy, properly nourished soul can exert this force, and the Christ-life within us needs its own particular nourishment to retain its resilience and vigor. It surely follows then that to receive with faith this Holy Food is adding immeasurably to the health and strength of the innermost soul.

Christ and the Real Self

IT MIGHT BE questioned . . . whether we are to think of the Holy Food as nourishing the life of Christ within us or whether it is our own souls which are feeding on the "Bread of the world in mercy broken." Here let us put forward the bold suggestion that our "real selves," "our souls," and the "Christ within us" are essentially the same thing. We shall certainly find support for this view in the teaching of the New Testament. First, let us establish the fact that there is a "real self" within us all. If there were not, there would be nothing in Matthew, Peter, James, and John, and the millions since their day, to respond to the One Who says, "Follow Me." There is no need to stress here the reality of the other factors within us; we are only too well aware of them. But it would appear from the record of the Gospels that Christ invariably addressed Himself to the real person existing behind the facade presented to the world. Even His scathing onslaughts against the hypocrisy of the religious leaders may fairly be regarded as an "armor-piercing" method designed to reach the diminished but real person within.

Now, when that real person, either suddenly or gradually, decides to follow Christ, he experiences not only a sense of peace, forgiveness, and deep happiness, but also of being, in a previously unimagined way, in touch with the Infinite God. Small, poor, and flickering his flame may be, but in all humility he recognizes that it is a tiny part of the celestial Radiance.

Christ Himself plainly taught that His own life and those

of His close disciples were interwoven not only with each other but even with the eternal life of the Father. Familiarity has dulled for most of us that hitherto unheard-of intimacy between the life of God, the life of Christ, and the life of the disciples of Christ, which is spoken of as a plain matter of fact in, for example, Chapters 14, 15, and 16 of St. John's Gospel. Like many other of the New Testament promises, we tend to think of these things as too good to be true, and cannot see that they are both good and true. The life of the Vine, for example, and the life of the branches is of the same stuff, essence, and quality. It cannot therefore be impertinent for us to hold firmly to the belief that the life of our real selves is the same thing as the life of Christ within us.

The letters of the New Testament abound not with pious hopes but with audacious certainty. "Now are we the sons of God," "heirs of God and joint-heirs with Christ," "seated together with Christ"—these are the sort of expressions which sparkle on the sea of that early Christian confidence. God is now no longer aloof, separate—He is one with His sons. Confidence that man could never muster, certainty which he never dared to believe possible—all this and much more has come true in Christ, and shines from the pages of these unself-conscious writings.

But we, in our cautious reverence, forget how closely God in Christ has identified Himself with humanity. Because of our worldly set of values, we set God on the wrong kind of pedestal, so that the reality of the Incarnation becomes as impossible to conceive as the thought of a company president having tea with his janitor! If we do that sort of thing, and ascribe this world's dignity and privilege to God (which is a frightful piece of impertinence), we miss the whole point of God's pride-shattering humility. But there is no blinking the facts. God *did* become Man, God *did* accept the limitation and frustrations of human living, God *did* link

Himself indissolubly with poor blundering humanity. He did not shrink from calling Himself, and acting as though He were, Representative Man, which is what "Son of Man" means. Moreover, in that picture of the Last Judgment, commonly known as the Parable of the Sheep and Goats, He so far identifies Himself with needy suffering human beings as to state categorically that the way in which men treat each other is in solemn fact the way in which they treat Him (Matthew 25:40–46).

In the light then of God's deliberate identification of Himself with mortal man through Christ, we shall not go far wrong if we identify the Christ Who is formed and is developing within us with the real self which has heard and is responding to His call. We need this particular nourishment, for upon the health of this vital center depends the whole quality of our life.

Physical and Mental Preparation for Communion

IF THIS IS an occasion when man can in a unique way make contact with his God and Savior (and surely it must always be such an occasion, even when we ourselves are weary and depressed), there must be a certain deliberate preparation of body, mind, and soul. No one, of course, makes any social contact without taking the trouble to prepare; how much more ready should we be to prepare ourselves to meet God at these special points in our earthly pilgrimage? Let us consider our bodies first. Surely the best way of setting either mind or spirit free is to be as unaware of the body as possible. If the body is overtired or out of sorts, it will be a drag upon the mind and spirit. We should be sensible enough to see that the body is in as good condition as possible, so that for the time being we may forget it . . . .

Again, in posture we should aim at that position of the body which allows both relaxation and alertness of mind. No one would dream of attempting to tackle a difficult personal problem or even of solving a crossword puzzle while in a cramped and unnatural posture. Why should we expect the spirit to rise and worship and adore if the body is hideously uncomfortable?

We need also, as we have already said, to prepare the mind. Probably one of the greatest things that we can learn to do is to learn a holy relaxation. Sometimes we are unaware of the cause of our tensions, but often they are revealed to us as we deliberately open our mental life to the Spirit of God. We may find that we have been trying to preserve an inflated idea of ourselves; we may find that we have been childishly nursing a grudge against life or against someone else. There are innumerable causes of tension, but in the presence of perfect understanding they can be relaxed. We may need to apologize to God or to other people, we may need an honest laugh at our pretentious selves, or we may need quite simply to hand responsibility, too big for ourselves, into the hand of God. To remove these tensions, possibly with the help of a trusted friend, is one of the essentials of preparation.

Having eased the mind of its strains, most of us need some central thought by which we can focus our attention during the time of Holy Communion. Obviously there are innumerable lines of thought which we may profitably follow. Here we suggest only a few.

(1) We may let our mind range quite freely over the vastness and complexity of God's wisdom and power,

slowly allowing ourselves to realize that such a God focused Himself in the historic Person of Christ. From this point we let our minds dwell on the fact that Christ instituted this particular Sacrament; that though He is all about us, and indeed within us, yet it was no "bright idea" of mankind but Christ's own purpose that He should give Himself to us in the mystery of the holy Bread and Wine.

(2) Sometimes we may think of the vast unseen world existing quite independently of the time-and-space setup. We may think of the times when spiritual reality touches us very closely. We may use our imaginations freely, and not feel in the least ashamed that "we that are in this tabernacle do groan being burdened." We may remind ourselves that though we are citizens of the heavenly country, yet for the most part we walk by faith and not by sight. Our moments of illumination are few, yet here, so to speak, is a guaranteed point where the eternal reaches through and touches the temporal. This Sacrament is a pledge from generation to generation, not only of the Love of God but of the everlasting nearness of the spiritual in the material.

(3) Sometimes we may think of ourselves, small and feeble as we are, carrying out, in company with millions of others, the Will of God in a world disrupted and disorganized. We think of ourselves together as representing Christ, however imperfectly, to a world desperately in need of the very qualities which He can provide. We think of our own deep need for the strength and vitality needed to represent Christ in our particular circle. We need the nourishment of Christ within, His very Personality potent and operative within our personalities. Then we think of what this Sacrament provides—the very nourishment, the very Presence we need, ready to be absorbed into our own selves.

(4) Sometimes we may think of the memorial aspect of the Great Sacrifice. We may have been guilty, as so many are, of allowing our own sense of sinfulness, or our own

limited ideas of justice, to caricature our idea of God. We may see Him again "advertised" in this Sacrament as infinitely patient, vulnerable Love. The particular Communion we are attending is one end of a thread which leads back over the centuries unbroken to the Cross of Christ. "God was in Christ reconciling the world unto Himself." We may long reflect upon God's almost fantastic generosity in making reconciliation by this personal action and at this personal cost. Have we by any chance been trying to worship the wrong kind of God?

(5) Sometimes we may reflect upon the nature of sacrifice. How often no lasting good is achieved without considerable cost to someone! We think of the lives of truly great men and women and how their great deeds have not influenced the lives of others without sacrifice. There is no need to be morbid, for often the sacrifices were cheerfully made. But it seems to be a principle of life that the lower must be denied to gain the higher, that no situation or person is redeemed without cost. Naturally we think of the One Great Sacrifice, now represented for us in poignant symbols in the broken bread and poured-out wine. We are to receive these things, this very Person, not only for our comfort and inspiration, but that we too may share, in a minor way no doubt, in the whole vast work of costly redemption. In our receiving of the sacrificial food there lies not only a deliberate allying of ourselves with the work of Christ, but an acceptance of the strength and joy to make whatever sacrifices come our way with courage and good humor.

These five suggestions are but a few of the ways in which we can deliberately turn our minds from their normal preoccupation with earthly activities and become receptive to the Eternal Purpose.

Spiritual Preparation for Communion

MUCH AS A tiny gland may affect the whole functioning of the body, so what goes on in his innermost soul will affect the whole attitude and activity of a man's life. Only God has access to this inmost soul, and He through His chivalry only by our permission.

But most of us, if we come to Communion at all, desire to give that permission. We want to be touched by God. We know only too well that we are soiled and weary, infected by the world around us far more than we care to be, and we want to be touched afresh with the never-failing Spring of Life Himself. How then can we prepare our soul?

(1) Without morbid "muckraking" we can freely admit our prides and cowardices, our lack of charity and the poor quality of our faith. Then we can accept the cordial of God's free forgiveness and reinstatement. There is no question of our deserving such generous love, but it is a fact of life of which we can be quite sure. Then, if we have first relaxed the mind, we can allow our inmost selves to be both teachable and flexible. It is the hardest thing in the world for some people to admit that they have been wrong. But we really shall not get far in the spiritual life if, in the presence of Infinite Wisdom, we insist on being always right! God is the only one Who is always right, and His ways, though firm, are much gentler than we may suppose.

(2) Then, without whipping ourselves up into a false state of emotion, let us be expectant. What the Bible calls

"faith" appears to be the essential link between the boundless resources of God and our own feebleness. The life of God within us is limited far more often than we know because we do not really believe in how much becomes possible through faith in God. "Faith" is often like a faculty which has grown atrophied through disuse. It is that function of ours with which we can touch and hold the love and power of God.

(3) Lastly, we can gently train our souls to respond to the Love of God. We cannot force our own souls to love or to be grateful towards God any more than we can force anybody else to feel love or gratitude towards us. But we can at least put ourselves in the way of responding to God's Love. We can meditate upon it, upon the Nature and Character of God as revealed by Christ, and we can deliberately associate in our minds with God all those lovely and heartwarming things which, despite the evil, adorn our common life. It is only love that can beget love, and self-giving that can stimulate self-giving. We cannot force the pace here, but we can quietly look upon what sort of Person our God really is.

Now, it is obviously impossible for most people who live busy lives to make an elaborate preparation for Holy Communion, however desirable that may be. But if there is no preparation of mind and soul, what should be a tryst with God will in most cases degenerate into a "duty attendance." Of course, if we imagine that Holy Communion is some kind of magical prescription which can be received in regular doses to maintain spiritual health, preparation would hardly be necessary. But because it is no such thing, because it is the using of our highest faculties and the possible touching of our deepest springs of feeling, there must be at least a simple preparation of mind and soul. There will be times, naturally, when through ill-health or fatigue or that deadness of spirit which assails us all from time to time, there will be little emotional content. But this need not mat-

ter if in all honesty and sincerity of purpose we have confidently kept out appointment with God.

The Sacrament itself will vary in its emphasis according
to different needs or temper or circumstances. Sometimes it
may be a tonic; sometimes it may be an inestimable refreshment, sometimes a revitalizing of the very springs of spiritual life, sometimes a glimpse of Heaven and an unspeakable joy, sometimes a renewal of dedication in deepest
fellowship and with the Unseen Presence, but always it will
be to those who love and believe an appointment with God.

Forgiveness and Forgivingness

ONE OF THE most astonishing things that Jesus Christ ever
said was that men cannot hope to be forgiven by God
unless they are prepared to forgive the people who offend
or hurt them. I sometimes think this very searching truth
has been soft-pedalled, but it's very evident in the Gospels.
Every time we say the Lord's Prayer we say, "Forgive us
our trespasses as we forgive them that trespass against
us," and Jesus added: "For if you forgive other people their
failures your Heavenly Father will also forgive you: but if
you will not forgive other people neither will your Heavenly
Father forgive your failures" (Matthew 6:14–15).

If we could only see for a moment how much God is
prepared to forgive us, and how comparatively little we are
prepared to forgive other people, we might have a good
laugh at ourselves, which would do us a lot of good, as well
as help us to know much more of what being at peace with
God means.

The Church

THE CHURCH BEGAN with the supernaturally inspired insight of Peter who cried, "Thou art the Christ, the Son of the living God" (Matthew 16:16). Up to that moment, if we may look at things reverently from Christ's point of view, there had been swirling tides of emotion among the people whom He met. Popular enthusiasm ran high; He was the great Healer, He was the wonderful Teacher, He was a reincarnation of one of the prophets of old. But all this was an unreliable floating tide of opinion. Then came Peter's inspired remark, and at once our Lord (God walking the earth as a human being) seized upon the solidity of real faith. "You are Peter, the Rock-man!" He cried out, in delight, I think, "and upon this rock I will build my church" (Matthew 16:18). To Christ's matchless insight here was the beginning of this worldwide fellowship of men and women of all races. Here was the tiny beginning of the society which would transcend all barriers of color, class and custom, yes, and even time and space as well. For Peter, in a moment of true faith, had seen who Christ really was.

To see and to recognize who Jesus Christ really was and is makes the whole vast work of rescue possible. Prophets, poets, idealists, all have their message to give, but until someone sees that God Himself has penetrated into human life at man's own level there can be no real beginning to the work of making men whole. Without this recognition there is no certainty, only a feeling. Without this recognition there is no observable purpose in all the ills and accidents, the injustices and the bitter disappointment in this transitory part of existence that we call life. But once this recognition has come to birth, the certainty is there, the guarantee is there, the power is there; the authority, the plan and the purpose are all there, and the building can begin. No wonder Christ said of Peter's outburst of faith, "upon *this* rock I will build my church."

Fellowship of the Church

IT IS VERY noticeable in the New Testament records of the early Church that Christianity existed in fellowship. Of course, it may easily be pointed out that a sect which was such a tiny minority in a pagan world would be forced to close its ranks and stand together if it were to survive at all. That is perfectly true, but it was surely more than mere expediency that kept the early Christians together. Surely part of their extraordinary strength and vitality was due to their being "of one heart and mind." They worshiped and prayed together; they shared in "the breaking of bread" (Acts 2:42). Even though, judging from the evidence of Paul's letters, it was not very long before factions and "splinter groups" arose, yet the overall picture is of the Young Church standing firm and fearless in fellowship.

Because human beings are for the most part gregarious by nature, they tend to join with others who have similar interests. There are clubs, associations, fraternities, and societies without number throughout the whole civilized world to join together in fellowship people whose common interest may be fly fishing, stamp collecting, bird watching, hiking, photography, gardening, interplanetary travel, or any of a host of widely assorted subjects. Since this is so, it would appear to the casual observer that the fellowship of the Church is simply another organization, in this case an association of people whose interests lie in the Christian religion. But this is very far from being the case, for the fellowship of Christians is the outward manifestation of a deep spiritual unity. Men and women have discovered through the living Spirit of God what they are meant to be and the Plan with which they are called to cooperate. They have discovered the reality of the spiritual order and, what is even more important, they have found that Jesus Christ is no mere Figure of history but a living contemporary Person Whose personality and power cleanses and invigorates their own. They have discovered beneath the surface of different temperaments and backgrounds that they belong to the same family—that they are all sons and daughters of the same Father. They are, in a world largely insensitive to the true order of things, "picked representatives" of the new humanity (Colossians 3:12). In a very real sense they are carrying on the work which Christ began so long ago, not so much in admiration and memory of Him, but as people dedicated to follow the leading of His contemporary Spirit. They form together, as Paul pointed out long ago, "the body of Christ" (1 Corinthians 12:27). They are not a human organization but a suprahuman organism. They are the life of the real world being expressed in human terms in the present temporary setup.

Of course, all the above may appear a pathetically or even a ridiculously idealistic picture of the modern Church. But surely the words fairly represent what the Church should be and could be, and they at least partly explain why Christian fellowship in the Church is far more essential than any human association for the promotion of this, that, or the other. Because Christians are "members one of another" they must work as an organic whole, different as their individual functions may be. All this means that a very large part of our Christian maintenance will consist of joining in with the fellowship of the Church, in its prayer and worship, in its work and service . . . .

If the Church is to make any worthwhile impact on the surrounding community, if it is even to speak with a voice worth hearing, it must have the active, committed support of all true Christians . . . .

This whole question of entering fully into the worship and work of the Church must be faced by all those who genuinely desire to serve Christ in this modern age. There is an immense amount of diffused goodwill and willingness to serve others in countries with a Christian tradition such as this. Such things are far from valueless to the community as a whole, but I am convinced they would be far more potent in coping with mankind's ills and necessities if they were part of the extramural work of the Church of Christ. The Christian Church should surely be the center of inspiration, as well as the meeting place for worship.

Christian Service

THE EARLY VIGOROUS Church was essentially a working, serving, and forward-looking Church. Partly because of a sensitivity to the Spirit's direction and partly because of the rising tide of persecution the Young Church did not have much chance of becoming self-satisfied and complacent. It expanded and spread into all sorts of unlikely places armed only with the Good News of the love and power of the Spirit. Throughout the New Testament letters we can see how insistent are Paul and the others that the love of God which has sprung up in men's hearts at the touch of Christ must be expressed in outward conduct toward a pagan and frequently hostile world. The early Christians were pioneers of a new way of life, and many of them plainly regarded themselves as expendable for the cause of the Kingdom. The time had not yet come for any church to become inward-looking, prosperous, or self-satisfied.

Sometimes nowadays one gets the impression that the Christian churches have largely ceased to look outward. It is almost as though Christians exist in a closed circle of fellowship, with all their members facing inward, while behind their backs there are the millions who long, albeit unconsciously, for the Gospel, and for the point and purpose in life that only the Gospel can bring. If the churches are to recover the vast power and influence of the Church of New Testament times, there must be a fundamental change of attitude in many churches, which means, of course, a fundamental change in the attitude of the churches' members. We must recover our sense of vocation, our sense that we are not, as I said above, an organization of people who have a common interest in religion, but the local representatives of the God Whom we serve and of the Heaven to which we belong.

We may be full of joy, but we are not here for our own amusement. We are here to be used as instruments in God's Purpose. It is a fine thing to know that we are "right with God," "converted," "born again," and all the rest of it, but after a while such experiences become stale and unsatisfying unless we are passing the Good News on to others, positively assisting the work of the Church, or definitely bringing to bear upon actual human situations the pattern of Christian living. This means in effect that each Christian must ask himself, "Am I myself outward-looking in my Christian experience, or am I content to remain in a safe 'Christian rut'?" The recovery of the Church's power rests ultimately upon the individual Christian's answer to such a question.

Coming down to actual practice, the Christian has to ask himself what he can do to express outwardly and effectively his inward spiritual certainty. Obviously his first duty is to live a Christian life in his home and in his place of work. This is where his witness is most effective, and frequently most difficult, but busyness in Church affairs is no substitute whatever for exhibiting Christian graces in the home or being known as a Christian in our place of work. But, assuming that we have seriously considered our ordinary Christian life and witness, we ought also as members of the Church to think seriously of what our contribution should be in terms of time, personality, and talent to the life of the church to which we belong. I have already referred to the horrifying paucity of *leaders* in most of our churches, of men and women who will take responsibility and work at a job for the love of Christ and His Church. The influence of the Christian fellowship upon children, upon adolescents, upon the community in which the Church's life is set would be vastly enhanced if even half the existing church members were to give a single hour of dedicated service every week to their church. Of course, to do such a thing even at the one-hour-per-week rate is costly, and a hundred different excuses crowd readily into the mind. But if the Church is to revive and become once more ablaze with the truth of God and full of the warmth of His love, its members must be prepared to meet the cost and make the sacrifice. The by-product will be of course the maintenance of a high level in the spiritual life of the individual members. For the real danger to professing Christians lies not in the more glaring and grosser temptations and sins, but in a slow deterioration of vision, a slow death to daring, courage, and the willingness to adventure.

I cannot refrain from bringing this to a personal point. Our gifts vary enormously; we cannot all be evangelists, pastors, or teachers. We cannot all be leaders or bear great responsibility, but there is certain to be something, some worthwhile piece of service, which only you the reader can do. It may be exciting, it may be humdrum, it may be participating in a new venture, or it may be a mere routine. The apparent importance of it does not really matter; what is of real consequence both to your church and to your own soul is whether you are willing to give yourself sacrificially.

Bible Reading

COUNTLESS MEN AND WOMEN throughout the centuries have found their inspiration and nourishment for the Christian life in reading the Word of God. Now, I am not at all sure that our modern way of living is suited to the old-fashioned methods of Bible study. It is not really going to help us to live today if we know, for example, the chronological order of the kings of Israel and Judah, or study verse by verse the book of Lamentations or the book of Esther. If we are pressed for time, and most of us are, what we chiefly need to do is to study the four Gospels and soak ourselves in their spirit, and then to study with imagination the Epistles or Letters, which reflect the life of the vigorous Young Church. I am far from writing off the Old Testament as useless; but to the modern follower of Christ, whose time is limited, it is infinitely more important that he should know intimately the four recorded lives of Christ and the message of the Letters of the New Testament than to possess cover-to-cover knowledge of the whole Bible, which is bound to be sketchy and superficial. To my mind the day of "proof texts" is over. It is not a matter of guiding our life and conduct by finding a particular verse or phrase. What is important is that we should really understand to the limit of our ability what sort of Person Christ was, what were His methods, and what were His aims. We need to know what He did in fact say about the important questions affecting life and death, which all of us have to face sooner or later. We need to use our minds, to be as unfettered as we possibly can be from prejudice and religious indoctrination. Let us see and feel for ourselves what Christ really was and really taught. Let us allow our minds and spirits to be thoroughly influenced, not by the traditions of men, but by what Christ Himself was, said, and taught. He is "the same yesterday, and today, and forever" (Hebrews 13:8), and as we read His recorded life we can reflect that it is not fancy but sober fact that He Himself stands beside us to guide and instruct us. We need His living Spirit to make the connection between the world of New Testament days and the world in which we have to live today.

This intelligent reading, particularly of the New Testament, will keep alive and alert our inmost spirits. The sacred pages are truly inspired, not I believe in any "verbal inspirational" sense but because they contain the Word of God or, in case that is a meaningless cliché, they contain truths of the Real World in the language of this. Again and again we shall find ourselves challenged, convicted, inspired, or comforted by truths that are not of man's making at all, but which are bright shafts of light breaking through into our darkness.

Christian Reading

IT IS A profound mistake to suppose that the Holy Spirit of God ceased to inspire writers when the New Testament had been completed. There are many Christians today who from one year's end to another never read a Christian book. They have little or no idea, for example, how Christianity is spreading throughout the world, of the triumphs and disappointments of the worldwide Church. They have given themselves no chance to know why there is a worldwide movement toward a once more united Church. They do not know the Christian answer to the challenge of Communism; they are even hazy about the very real and solid achievements of Christian men and women throughout the centuries. To be brutally frank, they are very ignorant both of the history and of the implications of their Faith. In other departments of life they may be highly competent, efficient, and knowledgeable, but over this, the very heart and center of their true life, they are frequently abysmally ignorant. These are, I know, harsh words; but the Church could be infinitely more powerful as God's instrument for the establishment of His Kingdom if its members were better informed in their minds as well as more devoted in their hearts.

Books, Films, and Plays

THERE ARE THREE main ways in which fiction (in which term we include books, films, and plays) can mislead us, and in consequence profoundly affect the idea we unconsciously hold of God and His operation in human life.

First, the tacit ignoring of God and all "religious" issues.

A vast amount of fiction presents life as though there were no God at all, and men and women had no religious side to their personalities whatever. We may for instance meet, in fiction, charming people who exhibit the most delightful qualities, surmount incredible difficulties with heart-stirring courage, make the most noble sacrifices and achieve the utmost happiness and serenity—all without the slightest reference to God. The reader is almost bound to reflect that all the fuss Christianity makes about "seeking God's strength" and so on is much ado about nothing.

Conversely, we not infrequently read of evil characters who, for all their lust, cruelty, meanness, or pride never seem to suffer the faintest twinge of conscience. There appears to be no spiritual force at work pointing out to them, at vulnerable moments, a better way of living; and repentance is unthinkable. The reader is again, unconsciously, likely to conclude that God does nothing to influence "bad" characters.

This bypass which neatly avoids God and the religious side of life is not characteristic perhaps of the very best fiction, but it is extremely common. In films in particular, with a few notable exceptions, "providence" is subject to almost cast-iron conventions. These include the socially desirable "crime-does-not-pay" ethic, and the inevitable happy ending. But any resemblance between the celluloid providence and the real actions of God in human affairs is purely coincidental.

In actual life, as any parson worth his salt well knows, ordinary people do at times consider God and spiritual issues. The evil, and even the careless, are occasionally touched by their consciences. Moreover, the tensions and crises which are the breath of life to the fiction writer arc the very things which frequently stimulate the latent spiritual or religious sense. It is an extraordinary phenomenon that the modern writer who has, Heaven knows, few reticences and who is sometimes almost morbidly analytical of his characters' actions, should so frequently use the bypass road round the whole sphere of a man's relations with his God.

Second, the wilful misrepresentation of religion.

It can of course be argued that it is no part of the duty of a writer of fiction to provide Christian propaganda—and that is perfectly true. But it is equally no part of his work, which is "to hold up a mirror to life," to give the impression that Christianity and the Church are no more than a subject for ridicule. It may of course be great fun for him—he may be working off a childhood grudge against an Evangelical aunt—to represent clergymen as comic, bigoted, or childishly ignorant of life, and Christians as smug hypocrites. He may even feel that there is more dramatic value in the rector who is a domestic tyrant or the nonconformist deacon who is a secret sadist than in the genuine articles. But he is not, in so doing, being fair to the actual facts of life, even though his writing my prove highly gratifying to the reader who is only too ready to welcome this endorsement of his own feeling that "religion is all rot anyway."

Again, this criticism cannot fairly be leveled at the best fiction, but it is extremely common in the popular type, and slowly but surely affects the conception of religion and of God in the minds of many readers.

Third, the manipulation of providence.

The author of fiction (and this is not the least of the attractions of authorship) is in the position of a god to his own creatures. He can move in a mysterious way, or an outrageous way, or an unjust way, his wonders to perform; and no one can say him nay. If he works skillfully (as, for instance, did Thomas Hardy) he may strongly infect his reader with, for example, the sense of a bitterly jesting Fate in place of God. He can communicate heartbreak by the simplest of manipulations, because he is himself providence, *but he is not thereby providing any evidence of the workings of real life.*

The whole tragedy of King Lear might be said to depend on Shakespeare's manipulation of the character of Cordelia. Because she is unable to see (though every schoolgirl in the pit can see) the probable consequence of her blunt "Nothing," the tragedy is launched. But it would be a profound mistake to confuse the organized disasters of even the greatest writer of tragedy with the complex circumstances and factors which attend the sufferings of real life.

Conclusions as to the nature of Life and God can only in very rare instances be inferred from the artificial evidence of fiction. We need therefore to be constantly on our guard against the "secondhand god"—the kind of god which the continual absorption of fictional ideas nourishes at the back of our minds. One tiny slice of real life, observed at firsthand, provides better grounds for our conclusions than the whole fairy world of fiction.

The Badness of Goodness

THERE IS A chapter in Professor Thomas Jessop's book *Law and Love* with the provoking title "The Badness of Goodness"; it explains with the utmost clarity why it was not the publicans and sinners, but those whose lifelong purpose was to lead good lives, who, by a strange paradox, became the deadly enemies of God in human form. It is, I think, a mistake to suppose that all the Pharisees, for example, were self-righteous humbugs whose unreality and hypocrisy Jesus mercilessly exposed. It would be truer to say that they were men ruled by principle, often with a great many conspicuous virtues; but they differed from Christ fundamentally in that the mainspring of their lives lay in observing the law and keeping their own souls unspotted from the world, while His lay in loving His Father with the whole of His being, and His fellow men with the same love that He

knew was eternally at the heart of His Father. Their religion
was a kind of contract, a *quid pro quo* performance, while
His was the spontaneous outliving of unadulterated love. It
must often have looked to them as though He were ready to
drive a coach and six through the law and the prophets. But
in fact He went far above and beyond any "righteousness"
that the law could produce. When directly challenged, He
declared that the whole of the prophet's message and the
law's morality depended upon the two most important com-
mandments, namely, to love God with the whole of the personality, and to love one's neighbor as oneself (Matthew
22:38–40). St. Paul, seeing the same truth in a slightly different way—and not, I think, ever quite able, despite his
protestations, to shake himself completely free from the
Law in which he was nurtured—declared, "Love therefore
is the fulfillment of the law" (Romans 13:10).

It would be a profound mistake to suppose that all the
Pharisees disappeared soon after the death of Christ, or that
they have no heirs and successors today. Indeed, it is true
that there is much of the Pharisee in each one of us, and by
that I do not mean that we are hypocrites, but simply that
we would rather reduce religion to a code, both inward and
outward, than take the tremendous risk of being invaded
by and becoming part of vulnerable but relentless love. We
do not have to look far to find Christians who have tamed
and regulated something that can in fact neither be tamed
nor regulated. We do not like risks; we do not like being
hurt or disappointed; and there is in us all something of the
spirit which would rather label and condemn and bewail
than love and suffer and perhaps redeem. We smile as we
read of Peter's attempt to regulate the illimitable. "If I have
got to forgive," he said, "could we not regard seven times
as the maximum?" (Matthew 18:21). But the same spirit is
in us, and perhaps we have not yet seen how vast and humble and magnificent and generous is the love of God, nor

have we realized that we are to be "perfect as He is perfect" (Matthew 5:48). Yet until we have some realization of this illimitable love of God, we shall never understand the conflict between "religion" and the Son of God, observed and recorded for our learning.

Competition in Goodness

IT'S A STRANGE thing, but a lot of people seem to imagine that life is a kind of competition in being good! They think that Christians and the people who go to church are saying to those who live without faith, without ever going to church—"Look at us, we're ever so much better than you!" Consequently, the non-Christian, the non-Church-goer, quite often says,—"I'm quite as good as So-and-so who calls himself a Christian and goes to church regularly." And then he thinks he's given a final and crushing reply to the whole Christian faith!

I really don't know where this idea of a "competition in being good" came from; it certainly isn't the Christian religion. After all, judging by ordinary standards, I can think straightaway of a dozen good decent people who would never claim to hold the Christian faith and certainly never go to church, and they're very nice people. At the same time I can think of an equal number of people who *do* hold the Christian faith and who *do* go to church. They're full of faults and failings, of which they're well aware and which they're trying to overcome with the help of God. And they're very nice people too!

This "competition in goodness" idea is really quite beside the point. The fact is that a lot of decent-living people never seem to have any need of God. While among any group of Christians you'd be bound to find people who have sought God because they needed Him, either because their own temperaments were too much for them, or because life faced them with overwhelming tragedy or difficulty, or simply because they found that, until they knew God, life was a pretty empty affair with no aim or purpose. The question of being "better" or "superior" to people outside the churches doesn't, in my experience, arise at all.

Evil

THE POWERS OF EVIL, whether outside or inside the human personality, are never nowadays taken to have any real existence. We willingly admit to being maladjusted or repressed or deprived, and we are quite willing to have psychiatry explain our delinquencies and sins, but we do not usually admit the existence of "evil." Now to men like Paul, John, Peter, and James right and wrong existed as surely as light and darkness. The Christian's way was a tough and difficult battle, and to win it he needed "the whole armor of God." Theirs was a spiritual struggle against the unseen forces of evil.

If we talk or preach today about the reality of evil, we are accused of "dualism," which is a technical term meaning that this world has really two gods, the God who is all that is good, and Satan, who is all that is evil. If one's critics mean that we believe in the permanent existence of Satan, the devil, or the powers of evil, they are wrong, for we do not. Once we have passed from this stage of existence into the one Christ has prepared for us, "Satan" ceases to exist. But for the time being, the power of evil to obstruct, confuse, corrupt, seduce, dissuade—all the unholy battery by which the Christian is assailed—is real, and is to be fought and defeated.

If someone cannot grasp how a fact of this life can cease to be a fact in some other mode of existence, we need look no further for an illustration than our own bodies. For the time being, they are real enough, and we must feed and clothe and wash and generally look after them. No one but a madman believes that his body has no reality, and even the strictest ascetic has to eat and drink unless he is bent on suicide. These bodies are real, but only temporarily so. As we have already seen, they are doomed to physical dissolution sooner or later. In another world they cease to be. So it is with the powers of evil. They are "temporary" in the sense that they are limited to this life, but to regard them as anything less than real in the here-and-now can be most dangerous.

All this is nonsense to the uncommitted agnostic, but it is sober truth to the man who is honestly committed to the way of Christ. I have never yet met a Christian who was not tempted, sometimes severely and for a long time. And I don't think I have ever met an agnostic who has any idea of what we mean by our battle against spiritual powers of evil. The New Testament view makes better sense to me than the best of humanism, as well as describing something far more like my own experience and that of the Christians I know. There *is* a struggle, sometimes a very bitter and difficult one, and it is not merely against "absence of good" or "ignorance" or "the amoral unconscious mind." Maybe it is against these, but the sense of conflict against actual evil which the Christian has to fight is as real in his experience as any other part of his observed existence.

Temptation

JESUS APPARENTLY SPOKE of "Satan," "the devil," "the prince of this world," and "the wicked one." Paul wrote of "Satan," "the god of this world," "the devil," and in the famous sixth chapter of his letter to the Ephesians he speaks of the battle of the Christian "against principalities, against powers, against the rulers of the darkness of this world, against spiritual wickedness in high places." Peter warned his readers that their "adversary the devil, as a roaring lion, walketh about, seeking whom he may devour." James gave the advice to "resist the devil, and he will flee from you." John refers several times to "the devil," the "children of the devil," and "the works of the devil," and in speaking of the Christian's battle, he reminds his readers that "greater is he that is in you than he that is in the world."

There is no need at all for us to revert to medieval crudity and to conjure up a whole picture gallery of devils. But it is quite as unrealistic to suppose that there is no adversary, no sower of doubts and fears, no tempter to corrupt our best endeavors. Jesus used the name Satan for this evil force, presumably because it was current in his day and his hearers would know what he was talking about. But, just as he never argued about the existence of God, so he accepted as a fact of life this evil power which can, at any time, destroy or corrupt. It is noteworthy that when Peter was once inspired to see who Jesus really was, Jesus congratulated him on the insight given to him, and almost at once rebuked him sternly as "Satan," for suggesting a course that would be contrary to the plan of God (Matthew 16:23). I quote here from a recent book: "Anyone who has ever tried to formulate a private prayer in silence, and in his own heart, will know what I mean by *diabolical interference*. The forces of evil are in opposition to the will of God. And the nearer a man's will approaches God's, the more apparent and stronger and more formidable this opposition is seen to be. It is only when we are going in more or less the same direction as the devil that we are unconscious of any opposition at all." [*Of Heaven and Hope* by David Bolt.] These sentences are completely true to my own experience of life and to that of my Christian friends and correspondents. The battle of which the New Testament speaks so realistically is still raging, and every Christian finds himself involved in it.

Guilt

WE ARE NOT concerned with artificial guilt or sin. . . . All religions, Christianity unfortunately not excepted, tend to excite in certain people an artificial sense of guilt, which may have little or no connection with a man's actual standing before God. Probably Pharisaism, which Christ attacked with bitter scorn, represents this tendency at its highest, but it is a mistake to think that Pharisaism disappeared after the death of Christ. The danger of such a system, and the reason why Christ attacked it so violently, is that its values are artificial. The proud and correct feel "right with God" just when they are not, and the sensitive humble man feels hopeless and overburdened *for the wrong reasons*. (Christ's little cameo of the Pharisee and the tax collector at their prayers is an unforgettable commentary on this point.)

Imperfection

WE ARE NOT concerned with mere comparison with perfection. . . . A great deal of the sense of sin and shame and guilt induced in certain types of people is simply due to their (imaginary) comparison of their human standards with what they conceive to be the Divine Standards. Of course they feel failures! You have only to raise the standard, and go on raising it, to make anyone feel a hopeless blundering idiot. This may be what we are in comparison with the wisdom of God, but, to put it at its crudest, it would be an extraordinarily ungentlemanly thing for Him merely to keep raising the standard! After all, it is a foregone conclusion that no man can compete with his Creator, and there is neither sense nor justice in thinking that the Creator intends His creatures to feel permanently inferior and humiliated compared with Himself! Yet this comparison, cloaked and disguised, is often made in a certain type of sermon and a certain type of religious book. But the feeling of hopelessness and inadequacy it engenders is quite wrongly taken to be "conviction of sin."

Humiliation

WE ARE NOT concerned with mere humiliation. Quite a lot of people, if psychologically tested, would react with resentment to the words "sin," "guilt," "disobedience," "punishment," and so on. This is by no means necessarily because their adult lives are so proud and complacent that they resent criticism, but because there still exists in their minds a tender, touchy area connected with the misdemeanors of childhood. Unless they were exceptionally lucky it is quite probable that, though they have long ago forgotten the circumstances, they still half-consciously remember the shame, rage, impotence, and humiliation of childish naughtiness and its punishment. It was not without strain and conflict that they won free from adult domination, and it *feels* to them like a voluntary resumption of the humiliations of childhood to confess themselves "guilty sinners." For a little boy to be smacked on his behind may be of little significance, but for an adult man to be beaten is an unspeakable degradation. It is of course not really a renascence of this childish guilt and humiliation that the reputable evangelist seeks to arouse, but he may seem to be doing so. To have a real sense of sin is by no means the same thing as being humiliated.

Sin

THE TRUE ADULT sense of sin, guilt, and shame, which contact with the real God appears invariably to arouse (though by no means always at once), seems to come along at least four different lines, which we will attempt to illustrate.

(1) We will suppose that a man who is rather proud of his ability to knock off a quick effective little painting discovers a bit of canvas fastened to a wall. For his own pleasure and the appreciation of his friends he rapidly paints in a bright,

effective, and amusing little picture. Stepping back to see his own handiwork better, he suddenly discovers that he has painted his little bit of nonsense on the corner of a vast painting of superb quality, so huge that he had not realized its extent or even that there was a picture there at all. His feelings are rather like what a man feels when he suddenly sees the vast sweep of God's design in life, and observes the cheap and discordant little effort his own living so far represents when seen against that background. That is real conviction of sin.

(2) To illustrate the second way in which a real sense of sin may come, we will use a story which we believe is true, though it has not been possible to check its source. A young man of the "incorrigibile" variety grows up work-shy, and by a certain native quickness of wit manages for years to escape serious trouble. His favorite saying is: "I live my own life, and I don't care tuppence for anybody." Eventually, however, his self-confidence overreaches itself and he is convicted of serious crime and goes to prison for three years. While in prison he is hard and quite unrepentant. "What I do with my life," he says defiantly, "is nobody else's business. I shan't make the same mistake twice." In due course he leaves prison and, since he has nowhere else to go, decides to spend a few nights at home while he "looks around." He hasn't seen his mother since he saw her, plump, rosy, and tearful, out of the corner of his eye, at his trial. But when the door of his home is opened to him by a worn, grey-haired old woman, he does not see at once what has happened. For a second or two he simply stares, then he cries, "Oh, mother, what *have I done to you?*" and bursts into the tears that neither punishment nor prison had ever wrung from him.

This story is simply an illustration of how a man may suddenly realize the hurt he does to others by his own self-centeredness. It does not, unfortunately, often happen that a man sees as vividly as in that story the consequences of his wrong actions. But when he does he may experience a genuine conviction of sin. When Saul Kane in Masefield's *Everlasting Mercy* had his eyes opened, he suddenly saw "the harm I done in being me." That is just it. When a man sees not merely that his life is out of harmony with God's purpose, but realizes that that disharmony has injured and infected the lives of other people, he begins to feel a "sinner" in earnest.

(3) To illustrate the next point we must tell a simple story which will no doubt make the sophisticated smile. Two young men of the same age choose divergent paths. A is determined to squeeze all the pleasure and enjoyment out of life that he can. B is equally determined to "get on." Despite the gibes of his friend, he attends "evening classes" and works hard in his spare time at his chosen subject. We will suppose that the friends go separate ways and do not meet for several years. When they do B has unquestionably "got on" and has a responsible well-paid position. A has advanced very little. His reaction on seeing B again may quite possibly be just unreasonable envy, but equally possibly A may say to himself: "What a fool I've been! What opportunities I threw away. B is *just the sort of man I could have been!*"

This naive little tale illustrates quite well how a genuine "conviction of sin" may arise. A man who has lived selfishly and carelessly meets someone who has plainly found happiness and satisfaction in cooperating with what he can see of God's purpose. The former may pass the whole thing off as a joke. "Of course, old so-and-so always was a bit religious"—but he may quite possibly see in the other man *the sort of person he himself might have been.* The standards he mocked and the God he kept at arm's length have produced in the other man something he really very badly wants. If his reflection is, "What a fool I've been," he, too, is beginning to get a genuine sense of sin.

(4) The fourth road along which the "conviction of sin" may come is rather harder to explain. It is really the discovery of the enormous and implacable strength of real goodness and real love. The insincere man hates and fears the real truth; the sexually irresponsible man affects to be cynical about real and enduring passion, but secretly he hates and fears it; the egocentric man hates and fears the incalculable force of the personality selflessly devoted to a cause. In short, self-centered and evil people really *fear* the good. They express their fear by mockery, cynicism, and, when circumstances allow, by active persecution.

Now when this sense of the strength of goodness and love touches a man, whether it be by someone else's life, by something he reads or sees, or by an inner touch in his soul, he is really convicted of sin. He knows that sooner or later the game is up—the Nature of Life is Good and not Evil. He suddenly sees that the goodness and love he has despised as weakness are in reality incredibly strong. Peter once felt this about Christ and in a moment of panic cried out: "Depart from me, for I am a sinful man, O Lord!" Some people, of course, succeed in keeping the fear of goodness (which is really the fear of God) at a safe distance all their lives, but they live in continual danger of reality breaking in. And when it does there will be a strong sense of sin.

Reconciliation

To ANYONE THEREFORE who takes the unique claim of Christ seriously it is of the very greatest interest and significance to observe how He dealt with the question of sin and man's reconciliation with God. The following facts emerge from the records:

(1) Christ very rarely called men "sinners" and as far as we know never attempted deliberately to make them feel sinners, except in the case of the entrenched self-righteous, where He used the assault and battery of scathing denunciation. (This, we may surmise, is an instance of what He saw to be a desperate ill requiring a desperate remedy.) Some evangelists, whose chief weapon is the production of a sense of sin, would find themselves extraordinarily short of ammunition if they were obliged to use nothing but the recorded words of Christ. This is not, of course, to say that the life and words of Christ did not produce that genuine sense of guilt and failure which it outlined above, but it is undeniable that He did not set out to impress a sense of sin on His hearers.

(2) We find Christ unequivocally claiming the right "to forgive sins," but the grounds on which the sin of man can be forgiven are not, in the recorded words of Christ, the conventional ones presupposed by many Christians. We find in Christ an intimate connection between the forgiveness of sins and the existence of love in a man's heart. "Forgive us our trespasses as we forgive them that trespass against us" is so familiar in our ears that we hardly grasp the fact that Christ joined fellowship with God and fellowship with other human beings indissolubly. "Except ye from your hearts forgive everyone his trespasses," He is reported to have said after a particularly telling parable, "neither will my heavenly Father forgive you your trespasses." Moreover, on one occasion he said of a woman who was apparently something of a notoriety that "her sins, *which are many*, are forgiven: for she loved much." It seems to me consonant with Christ's teaching to hold that love is a prerequisite of forgiveness, and I take His consequent little story to the Pharisee to be another of those apparent "non sequiturs" of which the reply to the question "Who is my neighbor?" is a classic example.

On the other hand, it would seem that there is a possibility of a man's putting himself outside forgiveness by the "sin against the Holy Spirit." This, from an examination of the context, would appear to be a combination of refusing to recognize truth and refusing to allow the heart to love others. If God Himself is both Truth and Love it would be logical to suppose that a deliberate refusal to recognize or harbor truth and love would result in an attitude that makes reconciliation with God impossible.

Now if it is true that God is both Truth and Love it will readily be seen that the greatest sins will be unreality, hypocrisy, deceit, lying, or whatever else we choose to call sins against truth, and self-love, which makes fellowship with other people and their proper treatment impossible. Forgiveness must then consist in a restoration to Reality, i.e., Truth and Love.

(3) We must now ask whether Christ had anything to say about the clamant question of "atonement" mentioned above. He certainly hinted at it. He spoke of giving his life as a "ransom for many," and at the last meal which He shared with His followers He spoke of breaking His own body and shedding His own blood "for the remission of sins."

Now it is surely possible that to this question of atonement (as to the question of surviving death) Christ, whom we are considering as God in human form, could give the best and most complete answer by actual demonstration. He personally, being both God and Man, effected the reconciliation that man alone was powerless to make.

There are innumerable theories centering around the death of Christ as the atonement for the world's sins, and many of them frankly do not commend themselves to the honest modern mind. May we suggest the following way of looking at the matter.

We have already spoken of the vicious sin-suffering-death circle in which the world is involved, and of the individual man's helplessness to free himself from the entanglement of his own wrong-doing, let alone cleanse himself from the cumulative infection of the world's selfish living.

Suppose now that God, who has become human and represents in one person both His own Godhood and Humanity, allows Himself, though personally guiltless, to be involved in the complex. God, now, who made the inexorable rules of cause and effect, deliberately exposes Himself to the consequences of the world's self-love and sin. Because He is God, to do such a thing once in time is indicative of an eternal attitude, and we view the Character of God in an entirely different light if we see Him not abrogating justice, not issuing a mandate of reversal of natural law and order, but overcoming a repugnance which we cannot begin to imagine by letting Himself *be* Representative Man and suffering in His own Person the logical and inevitable suffering and death which the world has earned. The Moral Perfection which a man quite rightly dreads, has deliberately consented to become under the limitations of humanity, the focal point of the assault of evil. We cannot imagine what this would involve, but even to begin to think that it might be true takes the breath away.

Christians believe that this act of reconciliation was the inner meaning behind the rather sordid historical fact of Christ's death. The unreality, the pseudoreligion, the bitter hatred, the greed and jealousy that lay behind the judicial murder of Christ were the mere *setting*. The *fact* would have been the same wherever and whenever Christ appeared: evil would clash with Incarnate Good, and whether it was a cross, a hangman's rope, a guillotine, or a gas chamber, Christ would choose to accept death for humanity's sake.

Christ's Act of Reconciliation

WE SHALL ATTEMPT here no theories of atonement, but simply record that it is a matter of indisputable fact that when a man sees that God took the initiative in establishing a *rapprochement* between Himself and Man and underwent the (for Him) indescribable ignominy of death, his attitude toward God is from then on profoundly changed. The inarticulate but incurable sense that "something ought to be done about it," to which we referred above, is almost miraculously set at rest. Though it may defeat his reason to define exactly what has been done, a man knows that the "something" has been done. The idea of God, which was almost certainly a discomfort and possibly a threat, however reason might argue the point, is entirely changed. The former inevitable Judge is seen to be Lover and Rescuer, and if the revision of ideas is at all sudden there is bound to be a considerable emotional release.

To assent mentally to the suggestion that "Jesus died for me" is unhappily only too easy for certain types of mind. But really to believe that God Himself cut the knot of man's entanglement by a personal and unbelievably costly act is a much deeper affair. The bigger the concept of God the more the mind staggers at the thought, but once it is accepted as true it is not too much to say that the whole personality is reoriented. For most men in whom a moral sense is operating at all, are, unconsciously perhaps, trying to "put up a case" to justify their own conduct. The effort may only rarely reach the conscious level of the mind, but it is there, and the real "conviction of sin" which we defined above, however much it may be held at arm's length, is always in the offing. To realize that the effort to justify oneself, the hopeless effort to repay the overdraft, can safely be abandoned, is an unspeakable relief. It was all based on a false idea, that the central confidence of life should be in the self. It is a blow to the face of pride and a wrench to the habits of the mind to transfer that central confidence to the One Real Perfect Man, who was, and is, also God. But if the changeover is effected the relief and release are enormous, and energy formerly repressed is set free. This is what the New Testament means by being saved by faith in Christ.

This is, of course, far from being mere theory. People in all ages, of all nations, and of widely differing temperaments, have reacted in much the same way to Christ's Act of Reconciliation. Indeed so great is the weight of evidence that it would be sensible to admit that, if we cannot understand what happened and are at a loss to explain it, there is a mystery here beyond our powers of definition. We might even have the humility to say that God-become-man did something incalculable, the greatness of which we can only appreciate in a very limited degree.

But, though we may well be awed, we need not cease to use our minds, and we cannot but admire the superb psychological accuracy with which this Act was designed to touch the characters of men. Those who already to some extent live in love and truth will see the force and point of the Act almost intuitively. Those who are set, however secretly, in pride and self-love, will see nothing to marvel at and little to admire—though the Act may haunt them strangely as though it were the key to some long-forgotten door into life's real meaning. It is those who realize their spiritual poverty who find in Christ's Act the way into fellowship with God: it is the "rich" who are "turned empty away."

Nevertheless, although we have here a touchstone to reveal existing character, we have a great deal more than that.

Should the proud and self-loving man once see that God is *like that,* there may be, and sometimes is, a revolution in his whole scale of values. Should the careless-living man once see that this Act is a crystallizing in time of what is always happening—that every kind of sin, including apathy, is at heart seeking to destroy God—he too may see life with very different eyes. God may thunder His commands from Mount Sinai and men may fear, yet remain at heart exactly as they were before. But let a man once see his God down in the arena as a Man, suffering, tempted, sweating, and agonized—finally dying a criminal's death, he is a hard man indeed who is untouched. For Christ's claim to be not only God but Representative Man has had an almost incredible magnetic power. Over nineteen centuries have passed since that judicial murder in that turbulent little country of Palestine, yet still men see the Death as a personal matter. It seems to be designed to meet their own half-conscious needs. "The Son of God who loved *me* and gave Himself for *me,*" wrote St. Paul, as though for the moment the Act affected him alone; but the words have been echoed unprompted by an imposing number since his day. So wide has been the acceptance of this reconciliation that we simply cannot easily dismiss it, particularly as the only possible alternative way of thought is a simple denial of the impasse which is a "fact" to every spiritually sensitive person.

Perfection and Perfectionism

SINCE GOD IS Perfection, and since He asks the complete loyalty of His creatures, then the best way of serving, pleasing, and worshipping Him is to set up absolute one-hundred-percent standards and see to it that we obey them. After all, did not Christ say, "Be ye perfect"?

This one-hundred-percent standard is a real menace to Christians of various schools of thought, and has led quite a number of sensitive conscientious people to what is popularly called a "nervous breakdown." And it has taken the joy and spontaneity out of the Christian lives of many more who dimly realize that what was meant to be a life of "perfect freedom" has become an anxious slavery.

It is probably only people of certain backgrounds and temperaments who will find the "one-hundred-percent god" a terrible tyrant. A young athletic extrovert may talk glibly enough of being "one-hundred-percent pure, honest, loving, and unselfish." But being what he is, he hasn't the faintest conception of what "one hundred percent" means. He has neither the mental equipment nor the imagination to begin to grasp what perfection really is. He is not the type to analyze his own motives, or build up an artificial conscience to supervise his own actions, or be confronted by a terrifying mental picture of what one-hundred-percent perfection literally means in relation to his own life and effort. What *he* means by "one-hundred-percent pure, honest, etc." is just as pure and honest as he sincerely knows how. And that is a very different matter.

But the conscientious, sensitive, imaginative person who is somewhat lacking in self-confidence and inclined to introspection, will find one-hundred-percent perfection truly terrifying. The more he thinks of it as God's demand the more guilty and miserable he will become, and he cannot see any way out of his impasse. If he reduces the one hundred percent he is betraying his own spiritual vision, and the very God who might have helped him is the Author (so he imagines) of the terrific demands! No wonder he often "breaks down." The tragedy is often that the "one-hundred-percent god" is introduced into the life of the sensitive by the comparatively insensitive, who literally cannot imagine the harm they are doing.

What is the way out? The words of Christ, "Learn of Me," provide the best clue. Some of our modern enthusiastic Christians of the hearty type tend to regard Christianity as a performance. But it still is, as it was originally, a way of living, and in no sense a performance acted for the benefit of the surrounding world. To "learn" implies growth; implies the making and correcting of mistakes; implies a steady upward progress toward an ideal. The "perfection" to which Christ commands men to progress is this ideal. The modern high-pressure Christian of certain circles would like to impose perfection of one hundred percent as a set of rules to be immediately enforced, instead of as a shining ideal to be faithfully pursued. His short cut, in effect, makes the unimaginative satisfied before he ought to be and drives the imaginative to despair. Such a distortion of Christian truth could not possibly originate from the One who said His "yoke was easy" and His "burden light," nor by His follower St. Paul, who declared after many years' experience that he "pressed toward the mark not as though he had already attained or were already perfect."

Yet even to people who have not been driven to distraction by "one-hundred-percent" Christianity, the same fantasy of perfection may be masquerading in their minds as God. Because it is a fantasy it produces paralysis and a sense of frustration. The true ideal . . . stimulates, encourages, and produces likeness to itself.

If we believe in God, we must naturally believe that He is Perfection. But we must not think, to speak colloquially, that He cannot therefore be interested in anything less than perfection. (If that were so, the human race would be in poor case!)

Christians may truthfully say that it is God's "ambition"

to possess the wholehearted love and loyalty of His children, but to imagine that He will have no dealings with them until they are prepared to give Him perfect devotion is just another manifestation of the "god of one hundred percent." After all, who, apart from the very smug and complacent, would claim that they were wholly "surrendered" or "converted" to love? And who would deny the father's interest in the prodigal son when his Spiritual Index was at a very low figure indeed?

God is truly Perfection, but He is no Perfectionist, and one hundred percent is not God.

Spiritual Vitality

IF A MAN accepts the fact that the Character of God is focused in Christ, if he accepts as true the Act of Reconciliation and the Demonstration with Death; and if he himself is willing to abandon self-centered living and follow the way of real living which Christ both demonstrated and taught, he is still not out of the wood. For he finds that apart from exceptional effort or spasmodic resolution he is not spiritually robust enough to live life on the new level. He simply has not got it in him to live for long as a pioneer of the new humanity. He can see that it is right, and he can desire, even passionately, to follow the new way, but in actual practice he does not achieve this new quality of living. He may blame his own past, he may blame the ever-present effect of the God-ignoring world in which he has to live, he may even reach the melancholy conclusion that it is all a beautiful theory but that it cannot be worked in practice.

This very natural impasse was, of course, anticipated by

Christ. He knew very well, for example, that the followers of His own day would very quickly collapse when the support and inspiration of His own personality were removed by death. He therefore promised them a new Spirit who should provide them with all the courage, moral reinforcement, love, patience, endurance and other qualities which they would need. A fair reading of the New Testament writings apart from the four Gospels shows plainly enough that this promise was implemented. Ordinary people were not only "converted" from their previous self-loving attitude, but received sufficient spiritual vitality to cause no little stir among the world in which they lived. It is a mistake to think that in general the receiving of this gift led to excitable demonstration. Its normal function was to produce in human life the qualities which Paul catalogues in Galatians 5: love, joy, peace, patience, kindness, generosity, fidelity, adaptability, and self-control. These are in fact the very qualities which men so easily "run short of," and which, taken together, comprise a character corresponding to the Representative Man, Christ Himself.

It is this invasion of human life by something (or Someone) from outside which the modern mind finds difficult to accept. We are all "conditioned" by the modern outlook, which regards the whole of life as a closed system. A great many things may happen inside that system, but it is unthinkable that the whole huge cause-and-effect process should in any way be interfered with from "outside."

But when we suppose, even only for the sake of argument, that the teaching of Christ is true—that this little life is acted against an immeasurable backdrop of timeless existence—it does not appear in the least impossible that under certain conditions of harmony between *this* faulty existence and *that* Perfection of Life, contact might be established. The result would be, to us, in the literal sense, supernatural. Indeed, we have already seen that a man may, even ac-

cidentally, come upon something of beauty, truth, goodness, or love, and find the "other end" is connected with
the Permanent. At such times the closed-system idea is
quite plainly inadequate.

Now we may wish, especially if we are more than a little
tired of the closed-system idea and faintly but definitely
conscious of the Real World, that these invasions might be
more frequent or more demonstrable. Nevertheless, this
much we do know, and can reasonably expect, that if a man
honestly wants to follow the way of Christ and, as it were,
opens his own personality to God, he will without any
doubt receive something of the Spirit of God. As his own
capacity grows and as his own channel of communication
widens he will receive more. John goes so far as to call this
the receiving of God's own heredity (1 John 3:9). This does
not, of course, turn a man into a spiritualist medium! The
man's own real self is purified and heightened, and though
he will come to bear a strong family likeness to Christ he
will, paradoxically enough, be more "himself" than he was
before.

We may here point out the great difference that has come
to exist between the Christianity of the early days and that
of today. To us it has become a performance, a keeping of
rules, while to the men of those days it was, plainly, an invasion of their lives by a new quality of life altogether. The
difference is due surely to the fact that we are so very slow
(even though we realize our impotence) to discard the
closed-system idea. We have so little of what the New Testament calls "faith." And since it is fairly obvious that
"faith" is the first requisite in making contact between this
and the Permanent World we can scarcely wonder at the
enormous difference in quality between first-century and
twentieth-century Christianity.

Without a power from outside, the teaching of Christ
remains a beautiful idea, tantalizing but unattainable. With

the closed-system sooner or later you have to say: "You can't change human nature." Ideals fail for very spiritual poverty, and cynicism and despair take their place.

But the fact of Christ's coming is itself a shattering denial of the closed-system idea which dominates our thinking. And what else is His continual advice to "have faith in God" but a call to refuse, despite all appearance, to be taken in by the closed-system type of thinking? "Ask and ye shall receive, seek and ye shall find, knock and it shall be opened unto you"—what are these famous words but an invitation to reach out for the Permanent and the Real? If we want to cooperate the Spirit is immediately available. "If ye then, for all your evil, know how to give good gifts unto your children, how much more shall your heavenly Father give the Holy Spirit to them that ask Him?"

The Spirit

THERE IS AN apparent capriciousness and arbitrariness about the working of the Spirit of God which laughs at our modern docketing. The Spirit, like the wind, said Jesus, "bloweth where it listeth" (John 3:8), and though we can fulfill conditions and, so to speak, set our sails to meet the wind of the Spirit, yet (to change the metaphor) we can never harness or organize the living Spirit of God. We are indeed sure of His gentle purpose, but the details of His plan lie beyond our understanding and it is at once more sensible and more fitting for us to cultivate a sensitivity to the leading of the Spirit rather than to arrange His work for Him!

This unpredictable and suprarational movement of the

Spirit is an element in God's working which makes the whole Christian enterprise on which we are engaged at once more exciting and more difficult. "There were many widows in Israel in the days of Elijah . . . and unto none of them was Elijah sent, but only to Zarephath . . . unto a woman that was a widow," said Jesus (Luke 4:25–26), and He offered no comment on the seeming arbitrariness of the Spirit's working. Those who are responsible for what nowadays we call missionary strategy have always the difficult task of keeping in touch with the tides and currents of the Spirit of God as He pursues His "immemorial plan."

Now this apparently fortuitous element in the grand work of redemption, and which incidentally can be seen on a small scale in the working of any local church in which the Spirit is operating at all, is singularly exasperating to the tidy-minded. What God works in one place or in one person ought, we feel, to work in all places and in all persons. But we are not dealing with, shall we say, an electrical circuit in which the power of electricity can always be relied upon to do the same thing under the same conditions. We are not using an impersonal force, and if there is any question of using, it is He who uses us and not we Him. God is of course really moving, with what, from His point of view, if I may say so reverently, I can only describe as celestial ingenuity. But to us, who at the most only know the superficial facts of the situation, His actions may at times appear arbitrary or even capricious. I do not think we need to go "all solemn" about this, or to overemphasize our own ignorance and sinfulness. It is surely far better to accept with good humor the situation as it is—that His thoughts are higher than our thoughts, and His ways higher than our ways (Isaiah 55:8–9); and to realize that though we are called to this tremendous task of cooperation with Him, and are no longer servants but friends, we still need to be most humble, teachable and flexible as we follow His leading.

Plain Christians

WHEN I TALK about the lives of plain Christians as being to me a proof of the reality of the Christian Faith, I am thinking of those who have taken that Faith seriously (and by that I do not mean solemnly!), and who have over a period of years lived their lives by that Faith. As a parson I am fortunate in meeting all sorts of people of all kinds of temperament, people of varying degrees of intelligence and in various walks of life; and the thing that impresses me about the genuine Christians is a certain quality of life which they all possess. It is rather difficult to put into words and, of course, I am not claiming that they are "saints" in the sense that they have no faults. But they all exhibit three particular characteristics which I think are quite remarkable.

The first is a kind of inward tranquillity, as though the very center of their personalities were relaxed and at peace. Many of them of course are busy people with all kinds of responsibilities to carry and often with heavy burdens to bear. But nevertheless they give me this strong impression that inside they are at peace—and that is a thing which I very rarely see in those without a religious faith.

The second characteristic which is common to all the best Christians is an unquenchable gaiety of spirit. Christians of course never expect, and certainly don't enjoy, any particular immunity from trouble; but I find in them the ability, not only to cope courageously with their particular difficulty, but very often to cope with it good-humoredly and even joyfully. I don't want you to think that I always and invariably observe this, but I must say that I have seen

not really in practice *enough* "niceness." What I mean is that they are charming and tolerant and kind within certain limits, but it is very, very rare to find them coping effectively with the messes and muddles made by the sins and failures of other men. Their goodness and their love are excellent up to a point, but they do not, as with the genuine Christian, enable them to cope effectively, and indeed redemptively, with a situation that has gone badly wrong. Of course I am not claiming that all Christians invariably do deal with dark and difficult situations effectually, but I do claim that the quality of their lives is such that something makes them want to move out from their own circle of love and happiness and bear some part of the pain and cost of putting a wrong situation right. They are not always very good at it, and they by no means always succeed, but for myself I am very much impressed by the fact that they do try to do something about it. They have, as I said before, an outgoing love.

The third weakness of nice people without faith is that they have literally nothing to offer to those who are *not* nice people. They probably behave kindly and tolerantly towards selfish people, but they have no means of communicating their secret of "niceness." To the man who has an unpleasant background, or an inherent moral weakness, they have no gospel to offer. They cannot, as the Christian can, point to Someone stronger than themselves who is quite capable of transforming a disposition and a character. The Christian knows God, or should I say a little bit of God, through Christ, and he has learned through his own experience to tap the resources of God. He can, therefore, at least point the way to a better quality of life to someone who is not by nature a nice type or a good type or an honest type. This the good man without faith is quite unable to do, since he has no experience of the active, operative power of God.

Christian Qualities

MAY I TELL you what I have observed of the quality of the life of the Christians that I have known? Naturally I have known a lot in the twenty-odd years that I have been a parson, and as far as outward circumstances, gifts and temperaments go, they have been a very varied bunch of people. Nevertheless, I am left with a very strong impression of a better quality of life lived by these people who have faith in God. I certainly don't mean that they are all perfect, or even that they are all saintly in the commonly accepted sense of that term. But, though they may be unaware of it themselves, their lives have got a quality—yes, I would almost call it a superhuman quality—which people who try to live without God never possess. There are many ways in which this shows itself, and I am only going to mention briefly four of them.

First, I notice that Christian men and women with a living faith in the living God have learned how the power of God can help them to cope with their own difficult natures. I don't claim that they always succeed, but I do claim that they know where to turn for spiritual reinforcement, and I do claim that in most of them you can easily detect something, or perhaps I should say Someone, operating in their own personalities who is higher and better than they would be by themselves. To put it quite bluntly, I have known people who would be called what we popularly term "nasty bits of work" if there were not operating in them Someone making them into good bits of work—changing them in fact

into sons and daughters of God. Even allowing for the failures, it is to me one of the biggest arguments for the existence of God that I see Him operating in lives which are
open to Him. I am not speaking of the super-pious, but of
the ordinary people who are open on the Godward side
and to whom marriage or home life or business life has
been made of quite a different quality by the unseen Spirit
of God.

In the second place I notice that real Christian people
have as a rule much more concern and much more love for
those outside their immediate circle. People living without
God are friendly towards those who are friendly with them,
of course, but usually their friendliness and concern only
operate within a very restricted circle. But when a man
opens his life to God, something of the Love of God comes
into his heart, and his sympathies grow both wider and
deeper. This is only perhaps what you might expect since
God loves every man, but it is wonderful to see how Christian people can give time and money and a very real love to
those who are quite outside their ordinary circle of acquaintances. It may be that they have a special concern for
the blind or other incapacitated people. It may be that they
have a special concern for those who have never heard the
Gospel of Jesus Christ. But the real point is that they have a
concern for the well-being of others, and I find this very
well marked in all true Christians.

The third thing that I must say about Christian people is
something in the nature of a tribute. Christians do not, as
some people foolishly suppose, imagine that they are spe-
cially protected from life's ills and accidents, from sickness,
bereavement, anxiety and all the rest. Indeed, it sometimes
looks as though some of the very best people get far more
than their share of misfortune. And yet I can't help observing (and this is where I pay my tribute), that these grand
people can bear disappointment and loss and ill-health and

all the other things that get people down, not only without bitterness but with the most astonishing courage and good humor. Again, I don't wish to make extravagant claims. They don't all do this. But I have seen so many of them living out the truth of St. Paul's words, "In all these things we are more than conquerors," that I am most profoundly moved and impressed. You see, theirs is not just a defiant courage, but that miraculous brave acceptance of the situation that turns a thing which is in itself evil into a shining beacon of faith and light and courage. Such grand Christians—and, thank God, I have met many of them—give the rest of us enormous encouragement.

The last thing I would say about people who live their lives with faith in God is that they have a Gospel to pass on. Many of them may be quite rightly reticent about their faith, for after all it is the most intimate side of their lives. But when the opportunity and the need arise, they can and do say something like this: "I know Someone far greater and stronger than you or I, Someone who has helped me through some pretty rough patches, and I am sure He can help you." And then sometimes they are able to show someone else, who up till now has lived life without God, how it is possible to get to know the infinite God through Christ, and how it is possible to tap His boundless resources through His Spirit who is living and active today.

Non-Christian Qualities

LIFE LIVED WITHOUT God is of poor quality. Now that is not a favorite theory of mine. It is a conclusion based on a good deal of personal observation. I expect you've realized that a parson has an almost unique opportunity of getting to know people, people of all types and temperaments, of all classes and of varying degrees of intelligence. Not many people have that opportunity. Most people know their own circle and have only the haziest idea of how other people live, except of course through books and films. People who live in towns have very little knowledge of how country people live, and vice versa. Business people, as a rule, only know their business friends and acquaintances, and a few friends outside. People who work in shops get to know their own customers pretty well, but they don't have much time or opportunity for knowing many other people apart from their own friends. But people like doctors, nurses and parsons, who are allowed into the homes of all sorts of people, have, as a rule, a much wider knowledge of human nature. They are privileged really, and when they have been on the job for over twenty years, working amongst different kinds of people, they can't help noticing a difference in quality between people who have a real faith in God and people who have not. Oh, by the way, I am leaving out . . . the hypocrites, of whom there are a few in any community, who pretend to be very holy and devout, and who are really thoroughly self-centered. I am thinking of the contrast that I have observed between the people who attempt to live without God and the people who have a living faith in Him. . . .

Let us look first at the people who have no faith in God. Please remember I am not condemning them; I am just telling you what I have observed.

The first thing I notice about them is that they have not got any real purpose in life. So often they are just waiting for something—waiting for the children to grow up and be off their hands, waiting for the time when they can retire. Very rarely have they got any sense of joining in and helping with a Purpose bigger than themselves. Many of them are very nice kindly people, but if you ask them straight out: "What are you living for?" they can usually give you only the most hazy or most trivial answers. I don't think they are aware of it, but to me it is pathetically clear that they are not linked to anything or anyone bigger than themselves.

In the second place I notice that such people have no one and nothing to turn to when they reach the end of their own resources. For example, a man may be cursed with a bad temper. He may know perfectly well that it worries his wife and frightens his children and spoils the atmosphere of his home. When he is pretty young he may battle against it and sometimes succeed, but as time goes on and he is defeated more often than not, he is very apt to conclude that there is nothing that can be done about it. His bad temper, or whatever the fault may be, is just one of those things that can't be altered. And so he shrugs his shoulders and simply makes a compromise with the bad temper or the jealous spirit or the bitter tongue, or whatever else it is that is spoiling his life. He does not know of any source to which he can turn which can enable him to control his own nature, still less to transform it.

Then too, I have noticed again and again that people who live without God are all right as long as they are well and reasonably prosperous, but that illness or accident knocks them completely sideways. Oh, they are ready enough then with, "How can there be a God to allow this to happen to me?" But they have never learned to find God as a refuge and a strength in good times as well as bad. Many of them are remarkably brave, but many more are completely lost when, for example, health fails, or there is some tragic happening in the family. They have literally no one to whom to turn.

The third thing that I notice about people who live without God . . . is that they have nothing constructive to offer to the men or women who are defeated either by their own natures or by the circumstances of life. Of course, they can and do say things like: "Cheer up—it may not be as bad as you think" or "Pull yourself together" or even, "Why can't you be like me?" but what they can never say, what they are quite unable to say, is, "I know Someone who is far stronger than you or I, who has helped me and who can help you." In other words, because they have no experience of God, they have no experience of any power or resource or refuge or strength outside themselves. And I think that is a very impoverishing thing.

Dark Tunnels

MOST OF US, sooner or later in life, have to go through what we might call dark tunnels, whether of pain, or adverse circumstances, or bereavement, or natural anxiety over someone we love. And when it comes we say to ourselves, "I do hope I shall come through this all right." But do we mean hope, real hope, or is that just a wish? Have we any reason, any good, solid dependable reason for hope? Can we, so to speak, see the light at the other end of the tunnel? Believe me, I do know what I'm talking about here and I can tell you that if your whole life is honestly committed, body and soul, to your creator, who is also your Father and your Savior—in the best sense your true lover—you can have real hope. You need not be lonely any more, and you need not be afraid any more, for you have not got to rely on the tension of your own screwed-up courage. You can relax, instead, upon the God of hope.

Once, some years ago, I myself went through a very dark tunnel indeed. And the words which came into my mind were these—"When thou passest through the waters I will be with thee, and through the rivers they shall not overflow thee." I rested my full weight on that promise and God brought me through that tunnel. A great many times since then I have passed that promise on to people in hospital or at home and, as simply as I could, urged them to rest their whole weight upon the goodness and the love of God. That is where hope, real hope, springs from. And Paul is perfectly right in calling God "The God of hope."

Darknesses and Depressions

I HAVE SUFFERED FROM ill-health during the last few years. To a large extent this was my own fault, for I accepted hundreds of demands on my time which were out of all proportion to my real strength. I should have realized that sooner or later a reaction was bound to set in. Therefore, I must say briefly that I now know a great deal about the assorted darknesses and depressions that can afflict the human spirit. And I know very well indeed how faith in oneself and one's own integrity, let alone faith in an omnipotent God, can be severely shaken and tested.

Of one thing I am quite certain. There is nothing that can help a man through a lengthy period of recovery better than a sustained faith in God, whatever one's feelings may happen to be.

I have read a great deal during the last few years, but I have never discovered anything that even remotely helps those who have to endure such times of depression unless it be found in, or derived from, the teachings of Jesus Christ and the New Testament generally.

Friends have helped in my period of depression, but I

have to say, in all honesty, chiefly those who have themselves suffered. And what are they but agents of the living God? I cannot bring myself to say that "suffering" is, by itself, a good thing. Yet it remains mysteriously true that those who have, through faith, conquered or come to terms with suffering are the only ones who can either understand or offer constructive help.

To go into all the implications of what I have hinted at here would require a book, and I doubt if I should ever be competent to write it.

But I see no hope at all in any view of life but the Christian one.

Inklings of Eternity

I HAVE *always* been aware of the eternal world. It often seemed to me that I lived in the here-and-now involuntarily and perhaps a little impatiently!

The innumerably clear and sharp experiences of childhood gave me hints and clues to beauty and reality which plainly transcended earthly life. I could not believe that this little life was my permanent home.

The sweetness of music, the loveliness of nature, the beauties of color and form were, at times, intolerably sweet reminders of some permanent reality lying beyond immediate perception.

Doors opened momentarily but would shut again tantalizingly. But those moments left a fleeting glimpse of unutterable beauty.

At the age of twenty-seven, these inklings of eternity crystallized in a dream or vision so real and so convincing that I can never forget it.

Let me tell you about it.

I had been vaguely ill for some months, and indeed had been forced to resign my first job through ill-health. I lay in a hospital, exhausted after a severe and prolonged operation. Physically I was weaker than I had thought it possible for a human being to be and yet remain conscious. I could hear and see, but I could not so much as move a finger nor blink an eyelid by any effort of the will. Yet my mind was perfectly clear, and late one night I overheard a doctor murmur to the night nurse: "I am afraid he won't live till the morning."

In my state of utter exhaustion, this aroused no emotion at all, but I clearly remember making a mental note that patients who are gravely ill and apparently unconscious may yet be able to hear.

I would not say that I felt then the presence of God as a person. I knew Him rather as some kind of "dimension."

I was however a helpless human being resting entirely upon my Creator.

God seemed to be, as it were, the sea of being, supporting me.

I felt that God to be infinitely compassionate and infinitely kind.

I fell asleep. Immediately, as it seemed, I had this startlingly vivid dream.

I was alone, depressed and miserable, trudging wearily down a dusty slope. Around me were the wrecks and refuse of human living. There were ruined houses, pools of stagnant water, cast-off shoes, rusty tin cans, worn-out tires and rubbish of every kind.

Suddenly, as I picked my way through this dreary mess, I looked up. Not far away on the other side of a little valley, was a vista of indescribable beauty. It seemed as though all the loveliness of mountain and stream, of field and forest, of cloud and sky were all displayed with such intensity of beauty that I gasped for breath. The loveliest of scents were wafted across to me. Heart-piercing birdsongs could be clearly heard. The whole vision seemed to promise the answer to my deepest longings as much as does the sight of water to a desperately thirsty man.

I ran towards this glorious world. I knew intuitively that there lay the answer to all my questing, the satisfaction for all that I had most deeply desired. This shining fresh world was the welcoming frontier of my true and permanent home.

I gathered my strength and hurried down the dirty, littered slope.

I noticed that only a tiny stream separated me from all that glory and loveliness. Even as I ran some little part of me realized, with a lifting of the heart, that Bunyan's "icy river" was, as I had long suspected, only a figment of his imagination. For not only was the stream a very narrow one, but as I approached it, I found that a shining white bridge had been built across it.

I ran towards the bridge, but even as I was about to set foot on it, my heart full of expectant joy, a figure in white appeared before me. He seemed to me supremely gentle but absolutely authoritative. He looked at me smiling, gently shook his head, and pointed me back to the miserable slope down which I had so eagerly run.

I have never known such bitter disappointment, and although I turned obediently, I could not help bursting into tears. This passionate weeping must have awakened me, for the next thing that I remember was the figure of the night nurse bending over me and saying, rather reproachfully: "What are you crying for? You've come through tonight— now you're going to live!"

But my heart was too full of the vision for me to make any reply.

What could I say to someone who had not seen what I had seen?

It is nearly forty years since the night of that dream, but I can only say that it remains as true and as clear to me today as it was then.

Words are almost useless as a means to describe what I saw and felt, even though I have attempted to use them.

I can only record my conviction that I saw reality that night, the bright sparkling fringe of the world that is eternal.

The vision has never faded.

Funerals

I HAVE TAKEN OVER 5,000 funerals. Though, of course, many of the mourners on such occasions have a very sketchy faith, even in the case of those who are convinced Christians of some years' standing, I find a strange inability to grasp the transitory nature of our present life and the breathtaking magnificence of the life which is to come.

I have, for instance, frequently suggested that it would be more appropriate to refer to the one whose physical body has died as the "arrived" rather than as the "departed."

No doubt there is nothing particularly original about this, but the significance lies in the fact that to many Christian people this is quite a new thought! They simply have not considered, or so it appears, that we are living this painful and difficult life against a background of unimaginable splendor.

Most of them hold desperately to a belief of some kind of survival, but that "the sufferings of this present time are not worthy to be compared with the glory that shall be revealed in us" seems hardly to have entered their hearts and minds.

Eschatology, Realized and Unrealized

"ESCHATOLOGY" IS THE doctrine or teaching about "the last things"—death, judgment, heaven and hell. Much of today's Christianity is almost completely earthbound, and the words of Jesus about what follows this life are scarcely studied at all. This, I believe, is partly due to man's enormous technical successes, which make him feel master of the human situation. But it is also partly due to our scholars and experts. By the time they have finished with their dissection of the New Testament and with their explaining away as "myth" all that they find disquieting or unacceptable to the modern mind, the Christian way of life is little more than humanism with a slight tinge of religion. For it is not only advertisers who attempt to deaden our critical faculties by clever words, there are New Testament scholars who, whether consciously or not, do the same thing. Thus, if you are to be thought up-to-date and "with it," you are expected to believe in current phrases. One of these is "realized eschatology," which means that all those things which Jesus foretold have happened, either at the destruction of Jerusalem in A.D. 70 or in the persecutions of the Church. In other words, the prophetic element in the teaching of Jesus is of no value at all to us in the twentieth century. Such a judgment makes Jesus less of a prophet than Amos, Isaiah, Micah, Jeremiah, and the rest. I find myself quite unable to accept this. There *is* an element of the prophecy of Jerusalem's terrible downfall and of the desecration of the

Temple—the horror of which we who are not Jews find hard
to appreciate. But the prophetic vision goes far beyond this.
It envisages the end of the life of humanity on this planet,
when, so to speak, eternity irrupts into time. There is no
time scale: there is rarely such an earthbound factor in prophetic vision. The prophet sees the truth in compelling
terms, but he cannot tell the day or the hour of any event,
still less the time of the final end of the whole human affair.

We are ourselves somewhere in the vast worldwide vision which Jesus foresaw, and for all we know, we may be
near the end of all things. You simply cannot read the New
Testament fairly and come to the conclusion that the world
is going to become better and better, happier and happier,
until at last God congratulates mankind on the splendid job
they have made of it! Quite the contrary is true; not only
Jesus but Paul, Peter, John, and the rest never seriously
considered human perfectibility in the short span of earthly
life. This is the preparation, the training ground, the place
where God begins His work of making us into what He
wants us to be. But it is not our home. We are warned again
and again not to value this world as a permanency. Neither
our security nor our true wealth are rooted in this passing
life. We are strangers and pilgrims, and while we are under
the pressure of love to do all that we can to help our fellows,
we should not expect a world which is largely God-resisting
to become some earthly paradise. All this may sound un-
bearably old-fashioned, but this is the view of the New Testament as a whole.

In a true and real sense the Kingdom of God was already
established upon earth, but none of the New Testament
writers expects the vast work of redeeming the whole world
to take place either easily or quickly.

Some, at least, of the early Christians apparently expected
the return of their risen Lord in power in a very short time,
and both Peter and Paul had to remind their converts that

the "time" was entirely a matter of God's choosing. Meanwhile the Christian life must be led with patience and courage, the true gospel must be proclaimed, and Christian worship continued. The light must shine in a dark and cruel world.

It might be thought that if a Man's hope and treasure lay in another, unseen world, he would have little contact with, or interest in, the world in which he is only a temporary resident. Of course there have been, and are, sects who live apart from the world, but that is not the general picture. It is not usually the atheists and agnostics who are to be found fighting disease, ignorance, and fear in the most dangerous and difficult parts of the world. And this is because the Christian faith, although inevitably rooted in "heaven," is incurably earthly. The seeds of this paradoxical attitude are scattered throughout the New Testament. "Religion" which does not express itself in compassion is a dead and, indeed, a dangerous thing. Yet the root of the relief of disease, the removal of ignorance, and the teaching of faith lies in the love of God. We love because God first loved us.

I feel I must stress this point because we seem to live in an atmosphere of "either/or," whereas it is really a matter of "both/and." Certainly it is useless to preach a gospel of the soul's redemption to a starving man. But it is equally valueless (and the world around us is full of examples) to make man affluent in this world and at the same time deprive him of any sense of God or of any meaningful life after death. "Compassion" and "charity" are both popular words today, while faith in God is regarded as largely irrelevant. But in fact both compassion and charity can be monstrously misused unless they are informed by the love of God. Hence we get situations in which compassion goes out to the violent thug who assaults an old lady for her meager savings, but none at all to her! Charity means instant social acceptance for the adulterer but little compassion for his deceived and deprived wife. To love God is the first and greatest commandment, said Jesus, and this is the priority insisted on throughout the New Testament.

Life After Death

THE "FOCUSED" God, Jesus Christ, revealed to man not merely adequate working-instructions for meeting life happily and constructively, but also the means by which he could be linked with the timeless Life of God. "Heaven" is not, so to speak, the reward for "being a good boy" (though many people seem to think so), but is the continuation and expansion of a quality of life which begins when a man's central confidence is transferred from himself to God-become-man. This "faith" links him here and now with truth and love, and it is significant that Jesus Christ on more than one occasion is reported to have spoken of "eternal life" as being entered into *now*, though plainly to extend without limitation after the present incident that we call life. The man who believes in the authenticity of His message and puts his confidence in it already possesses the quality of "eternal life" (John 3:36, 5:24, 6:47, etc.). He comes to bring men not merely "life," but life of a deeper and more enduring quality (John 10:10, 10:28, 17:3, etc.).

If we accept this we shall not be too surprised to find Christ teaching an astonishing thing about physical death: not merely that it is an experience robbed of its terror, but that as an experience *it does not exist at all*. For some reason or other Christ's words (which Heaven knows are taken literally enough when men are trying to prove a point about pacificism or divorce, for example) are taken with more than a pinch of salt when He talks about the common experience of death as it affects the man whose basic trust is in Himself: "If a man keep my saying *he shall never see death*" (John 8:51); "Whosoever liveth and believeth on Me *shall never die*" (John 11:26). It is impossible to avoid the conclusion that the meaning that Christ intended to convey was that death was a completely negligible experience to the man who had already begun to live life of the eternal quality.

"Jesus Christ hath abolished death," wrote Paul many years ago, but there have been very few since his day who appear to have believed it. The power of the dark old god, rooted no doubt in instinctive fear, is hard to shake, and a great many Christian writers, though possessing the brightest hopes of "Life Hereafter" cannot, it seems, accept the abolition of death. "The valley of the shadow," "Death's gloomy portal," "the bitter pains of death," and a thousand other expressions all bear witness to the fact that a vast number of Christians do not really believe what Christ said. Probably the greatest offender is John Bunyan, writing in his *Pilgrim's Progress* of the icy river through which the pilgrims must pass before they reach the Celestial City. Thousands, possibly millions, must have been influenced in their impressionable years by reading *Pilgrim's Progress*. Yet the "icy river" is entirely a product of Bunyan's own fears, and the New Testament will be searched in vain for the slightest endorsement of his idea. To "sleep in Christ," "to depart and be with Christ," "to fall asleep"—these are the expressions the New Testament uses. It is high time the "icy river," "the gloomy portal," "the bitter pains," and all the rest of the melancholy images were brought face to face with the fact: "Jesus Christ hath abolished death."

The fact seems to many to be too good to be true. But if it does seem so, it is because we have not really accepted the revolutionary character of God's personal entry into the world. Once it dawns upon us that God (incredible as it may well sound) has actually identified Himself with Man, that He has taken the initiative in effecting the necessary Reconciliation of Man with Himself, and has shown the way by which little human personalities can begin to embark on that immense adventure of Living of which God is the Center, death—the discarding of a temporary machine adapted only for a temporary stage—may begin to seem negligible.

We have so far spoken only of "death" as it affects the man whose inner confidence is in Christ, His Character, His Values, and above all His claim to be the expressed character of the Inexpressible God. There is no brightly cheerful note in either the Gospels or the rest of the New Testament for those whose real inward trust is in their own capabilities or in the schemes and values of the present world-system. It is (as St. Paul insists almost *ad nauseam*) only *"in"* Christ, *"in"* the Representative Man who was also God, that death can be safely ignored and "Heaven" confidently welcomed. We have no reason to suppose that death is anything but a disaster to those who have no grip on the timeless Life of God.

Communion of Saints

MANY OF US who believe in what is technically known as the Communion of Saints must have experienced the sense of nearness, for a fairly short time, of those whom we love soon after they have died. This has certainly happened to me several times. But the late C. S. Lewis, whom I did not know very well and had only seen in the flesh once, but with whom I had corresponded a fair amount, gave me an unusual experience. A few days after his death, while I was watching television, he "appeared" sitting in a chair within a few feet of me, and spoke a few words which were particularly relevant to the difficult circumstances through which I was passing. He was ruddier in complexion than ever, grinning all over his face and, as the old-fashioned saying has it, positively glowing with health. The interesting thing to me was that I had not been thinking about him at all. I was neither alarmed nor surprised nor, to satisfy the Bishop of Woolwich, did I look up to see the hole in the ceiling that he might have made on arrival! He was just *there*—"large as life and twice as natural." A week later, this time when I was in bed, reading before going to sleep, he appeared again, even more rosily radiant than before, and repeated to me the same message, which was very important to me at the time. I was a little puzzled by this, and I mentioned it to a certain saintly bishop who was then living in retirement in Dorset. His reply was, "My dear John, this sort of thing is happening all the time."

The reason why I mention this personal and memorable experience is that although "Jack" Lewis was real in a certain sense, it did not occur to me that I should reach out and touch him. It is possible that *some* of the appearances of the risen Jesus were of this nature, being technically known as veridical visions. But the writers of the Gospels, in their naive, unself-conscious way, make it plain that something much more awesome and indeed authoritative characterized Christ's "infallible proofs."

Second Coming

WE MAY FREELY admit that the early Christians were wrong in thinking that Christ would return in power within their lifetime. It is possible to detect in the writings of Paul, for example, a change of atmosphere in his letters to the Thessalonians (which were probably his earliest), and what is probably his last letter, the letter to Titus. But even in the latter Paul refers to the "looking for that blessed hope, and the glorious appearing of the great God and our Savior Jesus Christ" (Titus 2:13). The hope may have become deferred in its fulfillment, but it is still a very real hope. New Testament Christians may well have modified their early views as to the immediacy of Christ's return, yet the fact of His coming again in judgment of the world is always implicit in their thinking and hoping. We need to remember that among the early Christians were quite a number who were actually present when the Son of God ascended back to Heaven—a symbolic action, of course, but historically true. Such men would not readily forget the words of the heavenly messenger who told them quite plainly that "this same Jesus, which is taken up from you into heaven, shall so come in like manner as ye have seen him go into heaven" (Acts 1:11).

Unhappily for us, the whole subject of the Second Coming of Christ has been for many years the playground of cranks and fanatics. This has made us not only shy of dealing with the question ourselves but reluctant to believe in "the blessed hope" as a fact at all. Various people, especially within the last sixty years or so, have manipulated texts of Holy Scripture with little regard to context to prove that Christ would return on this or that day. For example, in my own experience I remember a man in 1934 hiring the Queen's Hall in London solemnly to warn the British Empire that Jesus Christ would return in Person on, I think, the 24th of June of that year. So convinced was he of his calculations that he stated at the time that if he were wrong he would "sink into well-merited obscurity." He left himself no loophole for later revision of the timetable as others have done, and I presume he still lives in his obscurity. This example is only one of hundreds of misguided people who have thought they could calculate what, on Jesus' own admission, was known only to the Father (Mark 13:32). But I really don't see why, because this important New Testament hope has been the stamping ground of the fanatical, we should be cheated altogether of what was essentially a part of early Christian teaching. . . .

Planners as we are, if we envisage the Second Coming of Christ at all, we see Him returning in triumph upon a scene already largely perfected. We think it would be a fine thing if the world were neat and tidy, all problems were solved, all tensions were relaxed, understanding and friendship were worldwide, health and wealth were at their highest peak, when Christ returned, not this time as a helpless babe, but as a King in power and glory. Of one thing we can be quite certain: this high, unfathomable wisdom of God works on quite a different plane from any human planning. The time of the irruption of eternity into time, the moment for God to call the end to the long experiment that we call life, will not be made in consultation with human planners! Judging from His previous action in human history, God is perfectly capable of choosing an unusual and unlikely moment, as it will appear to human beings. Indeed, if we are to take the words of Jesus seriously, His return to the world or the winding up of the time and space setup, whichever way we look at it, is to be in the middle of strife, tension, and fear. In the letters of the New Testament it is the same: the coming of Christ is a blessed hope of intervention, not a personal appearance at a Utopian celebration.

Now if our hopes, whatever we protest, really lie in this world instead of in the eternal Order, we shall find it difficult to accept the New Testament teaching of the Second Coming. In our eyes the job is not yet done, and such an action would be, though we would not put it so, an interference. But suppose our hope rests in the purpose of God; then we safely leave the timing of the earthly experiment to Him.

After Nineteen Centuries of Christianity

CRITICS OFTEN COMPLAIN that if the world is in its present state after nineteen centuries of Christianity, then it cannot be a very good religion. They make two ridiculous mistakes. In the first place Christianity—the real thing—has never been accepted on a large scale and has therefore never been in a position to control "the state of the world," though its influence has been far from negligible. And in the second place they misunderstand the nature of Christianity. It is not to be judged by its success or failure to reform the world which rejects it. If it failed *where it is accepted* there might be grounds for complaint, but it does not so fail. It is a revelation of the true way of living, the way to know God, the way to live life of eternal quality, and is not to be regarded as a handy social instrument for reducing juvenile delinquency or the divorce rate. Any "religion," provided it can be accepted by the majority of people, can exert that sort of restrictive pressure. The religion of Jesus Christ changes people (if they are willing to pay the price of being changed) so that they quite naturally and normally live as "sons and daughters of God," and of course they exert an excellent influence on the community. But if real Christianity fails, it fails for the same reasons that Christ failed—and any condemnation rightly falls on the world which rejects both Him and it.

New Testament Christianity

IF NEW TESTAMENT Christianity is to reappear today with its power and joy and courage, men must recapture the basic conviction that this is a Visited Planet. It is not enough to express formal belief in the "Incarnation" or in the "Divinity of Christ"; the staggering truth must be accepted afresh that in this vast mysterious Universe, of which we are an almost infinitesimal part, the great Mystery, Whom we call God, has visited our planet in Person. It is from this conviction that there spring unconquerable certainty and unquenchable faith and hope. It is not enough to believe theoretically that Jesus was both God and Man; not enough to admire, respect, and even worship Him; it is not even enough to try to follow Him. The reason for the insufficiency of these things is that the modern intelligent mind, which has had its horizons widened in dozens of different ways, has got to be shocked afresh by the audacious central Fact that as a sober matter of history *God became one of us.*

This primary Fact is the foundation of all New Testament certainty about God and life. But there is a second conviction which is almost equally important. For while it is true that the earliest Christians had personally witnessed the breakthrough of Eternity into time, they did not regard this as a solitary isolated action. The Young Church lived in the daily demonstrable conviction that this world was continually interpenetrated by the world of the Spirit. Indeed, though some of them had seen the Man Jesus ascend into the clouds before their astonished eyes, the fact that He was with them and in them became an increasing joyful certainty. To anyone who studies the book we call the Acts of the Apostles it becomes quite plain that the Holy Spirit is not a vague influence for good, not even just a powerful Wind of Heaven, but a Person with a purpose and ideas of His Own. The earth was once visited for a few years, visibly, audibly, and tangibly by God in human form, but thereafter it was (and, of course, is) continually subject to invasions by the Spirit of Jesus. Happily, the Young Church was sensitive, alert, and flexible, and we can read for ourselves to what miraculous triumphs the Spirit led them. Again, if we are to regain the buoyant God-consciousness of New Testament Christianity, we must not only accept afresh the planned Personal Visit but be ready for any number of subsequent invasions of the Spirit.

God's Comprehensive Love

WE MAY FIND IT difficult to hold all these thoughts in our mind simultaneously, but they fairly represent the way in which the New Testament writers looked at God, man and life. Paul, for example, with his Jewish upbringing and Pharisaic training, would have a higly exalted view of the one true God, but after his conversion he also knows that the same God whose wisdom is unsearchable is his Father, and he can speak personally and naturally of Jesus Christ as "the Son of God who loved me and gave himself for me." In my experience of people I have found that among committed Christians this "comprehensive" view of God both as the Creator of infinite wisdom and power and as the Father caring deeply for the individual is a quite ordinary phenomenon. It is the agnostic or the would-be atheist who produces and magnifies the intellectual difficulty. No one in his senses would pretend that God is anything but a vast unfathomable mystery, and nothing is more repugnant as well as impertinent than that attitude of overfamiliarity which suggests that we are now old enough to talk on equal terms with the Creator. Nevertheless, it remains true that a human being can in a real sense "know" God through Christ, and Christ himself can be truly alive to him. I have seen this recognition and knowledge of God in people of all denominations, in men and women of several different nationalities as well as in those who belong to various social strata. I have known extremely clever scientists as well as men of the highest caliber in literature or the arts who regard God with the deepest awe and at the same time know Him through Christ almost as a personal friend. I have also known people of a much simpler cast of mind, who would probably not be able to pass any formal examination, who have a sturdy and invincible faith in God their Father and similarly find Christ a real person. It is true that the comparatively unintelligent will sometimes use naive terms in speaking of God, but I have never found a true Christian without a profound sense of awe and wonder. I cannot help being impressed by what I have seen and by what people have told me. The laboratory check for spiritual experience is life itself, and it is exactly here, sometimes in the most appallingly dangerous and painful situations, that I have found faith both sure and radiant. In short, I have seen the experience of God described in the New Testament occurring again and again in our modern world.

Bibliography

The following is a list of J. B. Phillips' books published in the United States. When there has been a Macmillan paperback edition, the publication date appears in parentheses.

A Man Called Jesus: A Series of Short Plays from the Life of Christ. New York: Macmillan Publishing Co., Inc., 1959.

Appointment with God: Some Thoughts on Holy Communion. New York: Macmillan Publishing Co., Inc., 1954.

For This Day: 365 Meditations. Waco, Texas: Word Books, 1975. New York: Bantam Books, 1977.

Four Prophets—Amos, Hosea, First Isaiah, Micah: A Translation from the Hebrew. New York: Macmillan Publishing Co., Inc., 1963 (1969).

Good News: Thoughts on God and Man. New York: Macmillan Publishing Co., Inc., 1963.

The Gospels: A Translation into Modern English. New York: Macmillan Publishing Co., Inc., 1952.

Letters to Young Churches: A Translation of the New Testament Epistles. With an Introduction by C. S. Lewis. New York: Macmillan Publishing Co., Inc., 1957 (1960, 1968).

Making Men Whole. New York: Macmillan Publishing Co., Inc., 1958.

New Testament Christianity. New York: Macmillan Publishing Co., Inc., 1957.

The New Testament in Modern English. New York: Macmillan Publishing Co., Inc., 1958 (1965).

The New Testament in Modern English. Revised edition. New York: Macmillan Publishing Co., Inc., 1973 (1972).

Plain Christianity and Other Broadcast Talks. New York: Macmillan Publishing Co., Inc., 1956.

Ring of Truth. New York: Macmillan Publishing Co., Inc., 1967. Paperback edition, Harold Shaw Publishers, Wheaton, Illinois, 1977.

The Young Church in Action: A Translation of the Acts of the Apostles. New York: Macmillan Publishing Co., Inc., 1955 (1964, 1967).

Your God Is Too Small. New York: Macmillan Publishing Co., Inc., 1953 (1961).

Sources